C-4486   CAREER EXAMINATION SERIES

This is your
PASSBOOK for...

Child Care Worker

Test Preparation Study Guide
Questions & Answers

NATIONAL LEARNING CORPORATION®

COPYRIGHT NOTICE

This book is SOLELY intended for, is sold ONLY to, and its use is RESTRICTED to individual, bona fide applicants or candidates who qualify by virtue of having seriously filed applications for appropriate license, certificate, professional and/or promotional advancement, higher school matriculation, scholarship, or other legitimate requirements of education and/or governmental authorities.

This book is NOT intended for use, class instruction, tutoring, training, duplication, copying, reprinting, excerption, or adaptation, etc., by:

1) Other publishers
2) Proprietors and/or Instructors of "Coaching" and/or Preparatory Courses
3) Personnel and/or Training Divisions of commercial, industrial, and governmental organizations
4) Schools, colleges, or universities and/or their departments and staffs, including teachers and other personnel
5) Testing Agencies or Bureaus
6) Study groups which seek by the purchase of a single volume to copy and/or duplicate and/or adapt this material for use by the group as a whole without having purchased individual volumes for each of the members of the group
7) Et al.

Such persons would be in violation of appropriate Federal and State statutes.

PROVISION OF LICENSING AGREEMENTS – Recognized educational, commercial, industrial, and governmental institutions and organizations, and others legitimately engaged in educational pursuits, including training, testing, and measurement activities, may address request for a licensing agreement to the copyright owners, who will determine whether, and under what conditions, including fees and charges, the materials in this book may be used them. In other words, a licensing facility exists for the legitimate use of the material in this book on other than an individual basis. However, it is asseverated and affirmed here that the material in this book CANNOT be used without the receipt of the express permission of such a licensing agreement from the Publishers. Inquiries re licensing should be addressed to the company, attention rights and permissions department.

All rights reserved, including the right of reproduction in whole or in part, in any form or by any means, electronic or mechanical, including photocopying, recording, or by any information storage and retrieval system, without permission in writing from the Publisher.

Copyright © 2024 by
National Learning Corporation

212 Michael Drive, Syosset, NY 11791
(516) 921-8888 • www.passbooks.com
E-mail: info@passbooks.com

PUBLISHED IN THE UNITED STATES OF AMERICA

PASSBOOK® SERIES

THE *PASSBOOK® SERIES* has been created to prepare applicants and candidates for the ultimate academic battlefield – the examination room.

At some time in our lives, each and every one of us may be required to take an examination – for validation, matriculation, admission, qualification, registration, certification, or licensure.

Based on the assumption that every applicant or candidate has met the basic formal educational standards, has taken the required number of courses, and read the necessary texts, the *PASSBOOK® SERIES* furnishes the one special preparation which may assure passing with confidence, instead of failing with insecurity. Examination questions – together with answers – are furnished as the basic vehicle for study so that the mysteries of the examination and its compounding difficulties may be eliminated or diminished by a sure method.

This book is meant to help you pass your examination provided that you qualify and are serious in your objective.

The entire field is reviewed through the huge store of content information which is succinctly presented through a provocative and challenging approach – the question-and-answer method.

A climate of success is established by furnishing the correct answers at the end of each test.

You soon learn to recognize types of questions, forms of questions, and patterns of questioning. You may even begin to anticipate expected outcomes.

You perceive that many questions are repeated or adapted so that you can gain acute insights, which may enable you to score many sure points.

You learn how to confront new questions, or types of questions, and to attack them confidently and work out the correct answers.

You note objectives and emphases, and recognize pitfalls and dangers, so that you may make positive educational adjustments.

Moreover, you are kept fully informed in relation to new concepts, methods, practices, and directions in the field.

You discover that you are actually taking the examination all the time: you are preparing for the examination by "taking" an examination, not by reading extraneous and/or supererogatory textbooks.

In short, this PASSBOOK®, used directedly, should be an important factor in helping you to pass your test.

CHILD CARE WORKER

DUTIES:
Delegates duties as head of group for infant and toddler children of a child care center; performs related duties as required.

SUBJECT OF EXAMINATION:
The written test designed to evaluate knowledge, skills and /or abilities in the following areas:
1. Child development;
2. Fundamentals of child care;
3. Preparing written material; and
4. Supervision.

HOW TO TAKE A TEST

I. YOU MUST PASS AN EXAMINATION

A. *WHAT EVERY CANDIDATE SHOULD KNOW*

Examination applicants often ask us for help in preparing for the written test. What can I study in advance? What kinds of questions will be asked? How will the test be given? How will the papers be graded?

As an applicant for a civil service examination, you may be wondering about some of these things. Our purpose here is to suggest effective methods of advance study and to describe civil service examinations.

Your chances for success on this examination can be increased if you know how to prepare. Those "pre-examination jitters" can be reduced if you know what to expect. You can even experience an adventure in good citizenship if you know why civil service exams are given.

B. *WHY ARE CIVIL SERVICE EXAMINATIONS GIVEN?*

Civil service examinations are important to you in two ways. As a citizen, you want public jobs filled by employees who know how to do their work. As a job seeker, you want a fair chance to compete for that job on an equal footing with other candidates. The best-known means of accomplishing this two-fold goal is the competitive examination.

Exams are widely publicized throughout the nation. They may be administered for jobs in federal, state, city, municipal, town or village governments or agencies.

Any citizen may apply, with some limitations, such as the age or residence of applicants. Your experience and education may be reviewed to see whether you meet the requirements for the particular examination. When these requirements exist, they are reasonable and applied consistently to all applicants. Thus, a competitive examination may cause you some uneasiness now, but it is your privilege and safeguard.

C. *HOW ARE CIVIL SERVICE EXAMS DEVELOPED?*

Examinations are carefully written by trained technicians who are specialists in the field known as "psychological measurement," in consultation with recognized authorities in the field of work that the test will cover. These experts recommend the subject matter areas or skills to be tested; only those knowledges or skills important to your success on the job are included. The most reliable books and source materials available are used as references. Together, the experts and technicians judge the difficulty level of the questions.

Test technicians know how to phrase questions so that the problem is clearly stated. Their ethics do not permit "trick" or "catch" questions. Questions may have been tried out on sample groups, or subjected to statistical analysis, to determine their usefulness.

Written tests are often used in combination with performance tests, ratings of training and experience, and oral interviews. All of these measures combine to form the best-known means of finding the right person for the right job.

II. HOW TO PASS THE WRITTEN TEST

A. NATURE OF THE EXAMINATION

To prepare intelligently for civil service examinations, you should know how they differ from school examinations you have taken. In school you were assigned certain definite pages to read or subjects to cover. The examination questions were quite detailed and usually emphasized memory. Civil service exams, on the other hand, try to discover your present ability to perform the duties of a position, plus your potentiality to learn these duties. In other words, a civil service exam attempts to predict how successful you will be. Questions cover such a broad area that they cannot be as minute and detailed as school exam questions.

In the public service similar kinds of work, or positions, are grouped together in one "class." This process is known as *position-classification*. All the positions in a class are paid according to the salary range for that class. One class title covers all of these positions, and they are all tested by the same examination.

B. FOUR BASIC STEPS

1) Study the announcement

How, then, can you know what subjects to study? Our best answer is: "Learn as much as possible about the class of positions for which you've applied." The exam will test the knowledge, skills and abilities needed to do the work.

Your most valuable source of information about the position you want is the official exam announcement. This announcement lists the training and experience qualifications. Check these standards and apply only if you come reasonably close to meeting them.

The brief description of the position in the examination announcement offers some clues to the subjects which will be tested. Think about the job itself. Review the duties in your mind. Can you perform them, or are there some in which you are rusty? Fill in the blank spots in your preparation.

Many jurisdictions preview the written test in the exam announcement by including a section called "Knowledge and Abilities Required," "Scope of the Examination," or some similar heading. Here you will find out specifically what fields will be tested.

2) Review your own background

Once you learn in general what the position is all about, and what you need to know to do the work, ask yourself which subjects you already know fairly well and which need improvement. You may wonder whether to concentrate on improving your strong areas or on building some background in your fields of weakness. When the announcement has specified "some knowledge" or "considerable knowledge," or has used adjectives like "beginning principles of…" or "advanced … methods," you can get a clue as to the number and difficulty of questions to be asked in any given field. More questions, and hence broader coverage, would be included for those subjects which are more important in the work. Now weigh your strengths and weaknesses against the job requirements and prepare accordingly.

3) Determine the level of the position

Another way to tell how intensively you should prepare is to understand the level of the job for which you are applying. Is it the entering level? In other words, is this the position in which beginners in a field of work are hired? Or is it an intermediate or advanced level? Sometimes this is indicated by such words as "Junior" or "Senior" in the class title. Other jurisdictions use Roman numerals to designate the level – Clerk I, Clerk II, for example. The word "Supervisor" sometimes appears in the title. If the level is not indicated by the title, check the description of duties. Will you be working under very close supervision, or will you have responsibility for independent decisions in this work?

4) Choose appropriate study materials

Now that you know the subjects to be examined and the relative amount of each subject to be covered, you can choose suitable study materials. For beginning level jobs, or even advanced ones, if you have a pronounced weakness in some aspect of your training, read a modern, standard textbook in that field. Be sure it is up to date and has general coverage. Such books are normally available at your library, and the librarian will be glad to help you locate one. For entry-level positions, questions of appropriate difficulty are chosen -- neither highly advanced questions, nor those too simple. Such questions require careful thought but not advanced training.

If the position for which you are applying is technical or advanced, you will read more advanced, specialized material. If you are already familiar with the basic principles of your field, elementary textbooks would waste your time. Concentrate on advanced textbooks and technical periodicals. Think through the concepts and review difficult problems in your field.

These are all general sources. You can get more ideas on your own initiative, following these leads. For example, training manuals and publications of the government agency which employs workers in your field can be useful, particularly for technical and professional positions. A letter or visit to the government department involved may result in more specific study suggestions, and certainly will provide you with a more definite idea of the exact nature of the position you are seeking.

III. KINDS OF TESTS

Tests are used for purposes other than measuring knowledge and ability to perform specified duties. For some positions, it is equally important to test ability to make adjustments to new situations or to profit from training. In others, basic mental abilities not dependent on information are essential. Questions which test these things may not appear as pertinent to the duties of the position as those which test for knowledge and information. Yet they are often highly important parts of a fair examination. For very general questions, it is almost impossible to help you direct your study efforts. What we can do is to point out some of the more common of these general abilities needed in public service positions and describe some typical questions.

1) General information

Broad, general information has been found useful for predicting job success in some kinds of work. This is tested in a variety of ways, from vocabulary lists to questions about current events. Basic background in some field of work, such as sociology or economics, may be sampled in a group of questions. Often these are principles which have become familiar to most persons through exposure rather than through formal training. It is difficult to advise you how to study for these questions; being alert to the world around you is our best suggestion.

2) Verbal ability

An example of an ability needed in many positions is verbal or language ability. Verbal ability is, in brief, the ability to use and understand words. Vocabulary and grammar tests are typical measures of this ability. Reading comprehension or paragraph interpretation questions are common in many kinds of civil service tests. You are given a paragraph of written material and asked to find its central meaning.

3) Numerical ability

Number skills can be tested by the familiar arithmetic problem, by checking paired lists of numbers to see which are alike and which are different, or by interpreting charts and graphs. In the latter test, a graph may be printed in the test booklet which you are asked to use as the basis for answering questions.

4) Observation

A popular test for law-enforcement positions is the observation test. A picture is shown to you for several minutes, then taken away. Questions about the picture test your ability to observe both details and larger elements.

5) Following directions

In many positions in the public service, the employee must be able to carry out written instructions dependably and accurately. You may be given a chart with several columns, each column listing a variety of information. The questions require you to carry out directions involving the information given in the chart.

6) Skills and aptitudes

Performance tests effectively measure some manual skills and aptitudes. When the skill is one in which you are trained, such as typing or shorthand, you can practice. These tests are often very much like those given in business school or high school courses. For many of the other skills and aptitudes, however, no short-time preparation can be made. Skills and abilities natural to you or that you have developed throughout your lifetime are being tested.

Many of the general questions just described provide all the data needed to answer the questions and ask you to use your reasoning ability to find the answers. Your best preparation for these tests, as well as for tests of facts and ideas, is to be at your physical and mental best. You, no doubt, have your own methods of getting into an exam-taking mood and keeping "in shape." The next section lists some ideas on this subject

IV. KINDS OF QUESTIONS

Only rarely is the "essay" question, which you answer in narrative form, used in civil service tests. Civil service tests are usually of the short-answer type. Full instructions for answering these questions will be given to you at the examination. But in case this is your first experience with short-answer questions and separate answer sheets, here is what you need to know:

1) Multiple-choice Questions

Most popular of the short-answer questions is the "multiple choice" or "best answer" question. It can be used, for example, to test for factual knowledge, ability to solve problems or judgment in meeting situations found at work.

A multiple-choice question is normally one of three types—
- It can begin with an incomplete statement followed by several possible endings. You are to find the one ending which *best* completes the statement, although some of the others may not be entirely wrong.
- It can also be a complete statement in the form of a question which is answered by choosing one of the statements listed.

- It can be in the form of a problem – again you select the best answer.

Here is an example of a multiple-choice question with a discussion which should give you some clues as to the method for choosing the right answer:

When an employee has a complaint about his assignment, the action which will *best* help him overcome his difficulty is to
   A. discuss his difficulty with his coworkers
   B. take the problem to the head of the organization
   C. take the problem to the person who gave him the assignment
   D. say nothing to anyone about his complaint

In answering this question, you should study each of the choices to find which is best. Consider choice "A" – Certainly an employee may discuss his complaint with fellow employees, but no change or improvement can result, and the complaint remains unresolved. Choice "B" is a poor choice since the head of the organization probably does not know what assignment you have been given, and taking your problem to him is known as "going over the head" of the supervisor. The supervisor, or person who made the assignment, is the person who can clarify it or correct any injustice. Choice "C" is, therefore, correct. To say nothing, as in choice "D," is unwise. Supervisors have and interest in knowing the problems employees are facing, and the employee is seeking a solution to his problem.

2) True/False Questions

The "true/false" or "right/wrong" form of question is sometimes used. Here a complete statement is given. Your job is to decide whether the statement is right or wrong.

SAMPLE: A roaming cell-phone call to a nearby city costs less than a non-roaming call to a distant city.

This statement is wrong, or false, since roaming calls are more expensive.

This is not a complete list of all possible question forms, although most of the others are variations of these common types. You will always get complete directions for answering questions. Be sure you understand *how* to mark your answers – ask questions until you do.

V. RECORDING YOUR ANSWERS

Computer terminals are used more and more today for many different kinds of exams.

For an examination with very few applicants, you may be told to record your answers in the test booklet itself. Separate answer sheets are much more common. If this separate answer sheet is to be scored by machine – and this is often the case – it is highly important that you mark your answers correctly in order to get credit.

An electronic scoring machine is often used in civil service offices because of the speed with which papers can be scored. Machine-scored answer sheets must be marked with a pencil, which will be given to you. This pencil has a high graphite content which responds to the electronic scoring machine. As a matter of fact, stray dots may register as answers, so do not let your pencil rest on the answer sheet while you are pondering the correct answer. Also, if your pencil lead breaks or is otherwise defective, ask for another.

Since the answer sheet will be dropped in a slot in the scoring machine, be careful not to bend the corners or get the paper crumpled.

The answer sheet normally has five vertical columns of numbers, with 30 numbers to a column. These numbers correspond to the question numbers in your test booklet. After each number, going across the page are four or five pairs of dotted lines. These short dotted lines have small letters or numbers above them. The first two pairs may also have a "T" or "F" above the letters. This indicates that the first two pairs only are to be used if the questions are of the true-false type. If the questions are multiple choice, disregard the "T" and "F" and pay attention only to the small letters or numbers.

Answer your questions in the manner of the sample that follows:

32. The largest city in the United States is
    A. Washington, D.C.
    B. New York City
    C. Chicago
    D. Detroit
    E. San Francisco

1) Choose the answer you think is best. (New York City is the largest, so "B" is correct.)
2) Find the row of dotted lines numbered the same as the question you are answering. (Find row number 32)
3) Find the pair of dotted lines corresponding to the answer. (Find the pair of lines under the mark "B.")
4) Make a solid black mark between the dotted lines.

VI. BEFORE THE TEST

Common sense will help you find procedures to follow to get ready for an examination. Too many of us, however, overlook these sensible measures. Indeed, nervousness and fatigue have been found to be the most serious reasons why applicants fail to do their best on civil service tests. Here is a list of reminders:

- Begin your preparation early – Don't wait until the last minute to go scurrying around for books and materials or to find out what the position is all about.
- Prepare continuously – An hour a night for a week is better than an all-night cram session. This has been definitely established. What is more, a night a week for a month will return better dividends than crowding your study into a shorter period of time.
- Locate the place of the exam – You have been sent a notice telling you when and where to report for the examination. If the location is in a different town or otherwise unfamiliar to you, it would be well to inquire the best route and learn something about the building.
- Relax the night before the test – Allow your mind to rest. Do not study at all that night. Plan some mild recreation or diversion; then go to bed early and get a good night's sleep.
- Get up early enough to make a leisurely trip to the place for the test – This way unforeseen events, traffic snarls, unfamiliar buildings, etc. will not upset you.
- Dress comfortably – A written test is not a fashion show. You will be known by number and not by name, so wear something comfortable.

- Leave excess paraphernalia at home – Shopping bags and odd bundles will get in your way. You need bring only the items mentioned in the official notice you received; usually everything you need is provided. Do not bring reference books to the exam. They will only confuse those last minutes and be taken away from you when in the test room.
- Arrive somewhat ahead of time – If because of transportation schedules you must get there very early, bring a newspaper or magazine to take your mind off yourself while waiting.
- Locate the examination room – When you have found the proper room, you will be directed to the seat or part of the room where you will sit. Sometimes you are given a sheet of instructions to read while you are waiting. Do not fill out any forms until you are told to do so; just read them and be prepared.
- Relax and prepare to listen to the instructions
- If you have any physical problem that may keep you from doing your best, be sure to tell the test administrator. If you are sick or in poor health, you really cannot do your best on the exam. You can come back and take the test some other time.

VII. AT THE TEST

The day of the test is here and you have the test booklet in your hand. The temptation to get going is very strong. Caution! There is more to success than knowing the right answers. You must know how to identify your papers and understand variations in the type of short-answer question used in this particular examination. Follow these suggestions for maximum results from your efforts:

1) Cooperate with the monitor

The test administrator has a duty to create a situation in which you can be as much at ease as possible. He will give instructions, tell you when to begin, check to see that you are marking your answer sheet correctly, and so on. He is not there to guard you, although he will see that your competitors do not take unfair advantage. He wants to help you do your best.

2) Listen to all instructions

Don't jump the gun! Wait until you understand all directions. In most civil service tests you get more time than you need to answer the questions. So don't be in a hurry. Read each word of instructions until you clearly understand the meaning. Study the examples, listen to all announcements and follow directions. Ask questions if you do not understand what to do.

3) Identify your papers

Civil service exams are usually identified by number only. You will be assigned a number; you must not put your name on your test papers. Be sure to copy your number correctly. Since more than one exam may be given, copy your exact examination title.

4) Plan your time

Unless you are told that a test is a "speed" or "rate of work" test, speed itself is usually not important. Time enough to answer all the questions will be provided, but this does not mean that you have all day. An overall time limit has been set. Divide the total time (in minutes) by the number of questions to determine the approximate time you have for each question.

5) Do not linger over difficult questions

If you come across a difficult question, mark it with a paper clip (useful to have along) and come back to it when you have been through the booklet. One caution if you do this – be sure to skip a number on your answer sheet as well. Check often to be sure that you have not lost your place and that you are marking in the row numbered the same as the question you are answering.

6) Read the questions

Be sure you know what the question asks! Many capable people are unsuccessful because they failed to *read* the questions correctly.

7) Answer all questions

Unless you have been instructed that a penalty will be deducted for incorrect answers, it is better to guess than to omit a question.

8) Speed tests

It is often better NOT to guess on speed tests. It has been found that on timed tests people are tempted to spend the last few seconds before time is called in marking answers at random – without even reading them – in the hope of picking up a few extra points. To discourage this practice, the instructions may warn you that your score will be "corrected" for guessing. That is, a penalty will be applied. The incorrect answers will be deducted from the correct ones, or some other penalty formula will be used.

9) Review your answers

If you finish before time is called, go back to the questions you guessed or omitted to give them further thought. Review other answers if you have time.

10) Return your test materials

If you are ready to leave before others have finished or time is called, take ALL your materials to the monitor and leave quietly. Never take any test material with you. The monitor can discover whose papers are not complete, and taking a test booklet may be grounds for disqualification.

VIII. EXAMINATION TECHNIQUES

1) Read the general instructions carefully. These are usually printed on the first page of the exam booklet. As a rule, these instructions refer to the timing of the examination; the fact that you should not start work until the signal and must stop work at a signal, etc. If there are any *special* instructions, such as a choice of questions to be answered, make sure that you note this instruction carefully.

2) When you are ready to start work on the examination, that is as soon as the signal has been given, read the instructions to each question booklet, underline any key words or phrases, such as *least, best, outline, describe* and the like. In this way you will tend to answer as requested rather than discover on reviewing your paper that you *listed without describing*, that you selected the *worst* choice rather than the *best* choice, etc.

3) If the examination is of the objective or multiple-choice type – that is, each question will also give a series of possible answers: A, B, C or D, and you are called upon to select the best answer and write the letter next to that answer on your answer paper – it is advisable to start answering each question in turn. There may be anywhere from 50 to 100 such questions in the three or four hours allotted and you can see how much time would be taken if you read through all the questions before beginning to answer any. Furthermore, if you come across a question or group of questions which you know would be difficult to answer, it would undoubtedly affect your handling of all the other questions.

4) If the examination is of the essay type and contains but a few questions, it is a moot point as to whether you should read all the questions before starting to answer any one. Of course, if you are given a choice – say five out of seven and the like – then it is essential to read all the questions so you can eliminate the two that are most difficult. If, however, you are asked to answer all the questions, there may be danger in trying to answer the easiest one first because you may find that you will spend too much time on it. The best technique is to answer the first question, then proceed to the second, etc.

5) Time your answers. Before the exam begins, write down the time it started, then add the time allowed for the examination and write down the time it must be completed, then divide the time available somewhat as follows:
    - If 3-1/2 hours are allowed, that would be 210 minutes. If you have 80 objective-type questions, that would be an average of 2-1/2 minutes per question. Allow yourself no more than 2 minutes per question, or a total of 160 minutes, which will permit about 50 minutes to review.
    - If for the time allotment of 210 minutes there are 7 essay questions to answer, that would average about 30 minutes a question. Give yourself only 25 minutes per question so that you have about 35 minutes to review.

6) The most important instruction is to *read each question* and make sure you know what is wanted. The second most important instruction is to *time yourself properly* so that you answer every question. The third most important instruction is to *answer every question*. Guess if you have to but include something for each question. Remember that you will receive no credit for a blank and will probably receive some credit if you write something in answer to an essay question. If you guess a letter – say "B" for a multiple-choice question – you may have guessed right. If you leave a blank as an answer to a multiple-choice question, the examiners may respect your feelings but it will not add a point to your score. Some exams may penalize you for wrong answers, so in such cases *only*, you may not want to guess unless you have some basis for your answer.

7) Suggestions
    a. Objective-type questions
        1. Examine the question booklet for proper sequence of pages and questions
        2. Read all instructions carefully
        3. Skip any question which seems too difficult; return to it after all other questions have been answered
        4. Apportion your time properly; do not spend too much time on any single question or group of questions

5. Note and underline key words – *all, most, fewest, least, best, worst, same, opposite*, etc.
6. Pay particular attention to negatives
7. Note unusual option, e.g., unduly long, short, complex, different or similar in content to the body of the question
8. Observe the use of "hedging" words – *probably, may, most likely*, etc.
9. Make sure that your answer is put next to the same number as the question
10. Do not second-guess unless you have good reason to believe the second answer is definitely more correct
11. Cross out original answer if you decide another answer is more accurate; do not erase until you are ready to hand your paper in
12. Answer all questions; guess unless instructed otherwise
13. Leave time for review

   b. Essay questions
      1. Read each question carefully
      2. Determine exactly what is wanted. Underline key words or phrases.
      3. Decide on outline or paragraph answer
      4. Include many different points and elements unless asked to develop any one or two points or elements
      5. Show impartiality by giving pros and cons unless directed to select one side only
      6. Make and write down any assumptions you find necessary to answer the questions
      7. Watch your English, grammar, punctuation and choice of words
      8. Time your answers; don't crowd material

8) Answering the essay question

Most essay questions can be answered by framing the specific response around several key words or ideas. Here are a few such key words or ideas:

M's: manpower, materials, methods, money, management
P's: purpose, program, policy, plan, procedure, practice, problems, pitfalls, personnel, public relations

   a. Six basic steps in handling problems:
      1. Preliminary plan and background development
      2. Collect information, data and facts
      3. Analyze and interpret information, data and facts
      4. Analyze and develop solutions as well as make recommendations
      5. Prepare report and sell recommendations
      6. Install recommendations and follow up effectiveness

   b. Pitfalls to avoid
      1. *Taking things for granted* – A statement of the situation does not necessarily imply that each of the elements is necessarily true; for example, a complaint may be invalid and biased so that all that can be taken for granted is that a complaint has been registered

2. *Considering only one side of a situation* – Wherever possible, indicate several alternatives and then point out the reasons you selected the best one
3. *Failing to indicate follow up* – Whenever your answer indicates action on your part, make certain that you will take proper follow-up action to see how successful your recommendations, procedures or actions turn out to be
4. *Taking too long in answering any single question* – Remember to time your answers properly

IX. AFTER THE TEST

Scoring procedures differ in detail among civil service jurisdictions although the general principles are the same. Whether the papers are hand-scored or graded by machine we have described, they are nearly always graded by number. That is, the person who marks the paper knows only the number – never the name – of the applicant. Not until all the papers have been graded will they be matched with names. If other tests, such as training and experience or oral interview ratings have been given, scores will be combined. Different parts of the examination usually have different weights. For example, the written test might count 60 percent of the final grade, and a rating of training and experience 40 percent. In many jurisdictions, veterans will have a certain number of points added to their grades.

After the final grade has been determined, the names are placed in grade order and an eligible list is established. There are various methods for resolving ties between those who get the same final grade – probably the most common is to place first the name of the person whose application was received first. Job offers are made from the eligible list in the order the names appear on it. You will be notified of your grade and your rank as soon as all these computations have been made. This will be done as rapidly as possible.

People who are found to meet the requirements in the announcement are called "eligibles." Their names are put on a list of eligible candidates. An eligible's chances of getting a job depend on how high he stands on this list and how fast agencies are filling jobs from the list.

When a job is to be filled from a list of eligibles, the agency asks for the names of people on the list of eligibles for that job. When the civil service commission receives this request, it sends to the agency the names of the three people highest on this list. Or, if the job to be filled has specialized requirements, the office sends the agency the names of the top three persons who meet these requirements from the general list.

The appointing officer makes a choice from among the three people whose names were sent to him. If the selected person accepts the appointment, the names of the others are put back on the list to be considered for future openings.

That is the rule in hiring from all kinds of eligible lists, whether they are for typist, carpenter, chemist, or something else. For every vacancy, the appointing officer has his choice of any one of the top three eligibles on the list. This explains why the person whose name is on top of the list sometimes does not get an appointment when some of the persons lower on the list do. If the appointing officer chooses the second or third eligible, the No. 1 eligible does not get a job at once, but stays on the list until he is appointed or the list is terminated.

X. HOW TO PASS THE INTERVIEW TEST

The examination for which you applied requires an oral interview test. You have already taken the written test and you are now being called for the interview test – the final part of the formal examination.

You may think that it is not possible to prepare for an interview test and that there are no procedures to follow during an interview. Our purpose is to point out some things you can do in advance that will help you and some good rules to follow and pitfalls to avoid while you are being interviewed.

What is an interview supposed to test?

The written examination is designed to test the technical knowledge and competence of the candidate; the oral is designed to evaluate intangible qualities, not readily measured otherwise, and to establish a list showing the relative fitness of each candidate – as measured against his competitors – for the position sought. Scoring is not on the basis of "right" and "wrong," but on a sliding scale of values ranging from "not passable" to "outstanding." As a matter of fact, it is possible to achieve a relatively low score without a single "incorrect" answer because of evident weakness in the qualities being measured.

Occasionally, an examination may consist entirely of an oral test – either an individual or a group oral. In such cases, information is sought concerning the technical knowledges and abilities of the candidate, since there has been no written examination for this purpose. More commonly, however, an oral test is used to supplement a written examination.

Who conducts interviews?

The composition of oral boards varies among different jurisdictions. In nearly all, a representative of the personnel department serves as chairman. One of the members of the board may be a representative of the department in which the candidate would work. In some cases, "outside experts" are used, and, frequently, a businessman or some other representative of the general public is asked to serve. Labor and management or other special groups may be represented. The aim is to secure the services of experts in the appropriate field.

However the board is composed, it is a good idea (and not at all improper or unethical) to ascertain in advance of the interview who the members are and what groups they represent. When you are introduced to them, you will have some idea of their backgrounds and interests, and at least you will not stutter and stammer over their names.

What should be done before the interview?

While knowledge about the board members is useful and takes some of the surprise element out of the interview, there is other preparation which is more substantive. It *is* possible to prepare for an oral interview – in several ways:

1) Keep a copy of your application and review it carefully before the interview

This may be the only document before the oral board, and the starting point of the interview. Know what education and experience you have listed there, and the sequence and dates of all of it. Sometimes the board will ask you to review the highlights of your experience for them; you should not have to hem and haw doing it.

2) Study the class specification and the examination announcement

Usually, the oral board has one or both of these to guide them. The qualities, characteristics or knowledges required by the position sought are stated in these documents. They offer valuable clues as to the nature of the oral interview. For example, if the job involves supervisory responsibilities, the announcement will usually indicate that knowledge of modern supervisory methods and the qualifications of the candidate as a supervisor will be tested. If so, you can expect such questions, frequently in the form of a hypothetical situation which you are expected to solve. NEVER go into an oral without knowledge of the duties and responsibilities of the job you seek.

3) Think through each qualification required

Try to visualize the kind of questions you would ask if you were a board member. How well could you answer them? Try especially to appraise your own knowledge and background in each area, *measured against the job sought*, and identify any areas in which you are weak. Be critical and realistic – do not flatter yourself.

4) Do some general reading in areas in which you feel you may be weak

For example, if the job involves supervision and your past experience has NOT, some general reading in supervisory methods and practices, particularly in the field of human relations, might be useful. Do NOT study agency procedures or detailed manuals. The oral board will be testing your understanding and capacity, not your memory.

5) Get a good night's sleep and watch your general health and mental attitude

You will want a clear head at the interview. Take care of a cold or any other minor ailment, and of course, no hangovers.

What should be done on the day of the interview?

Now comes the day of the interview itself. Give yourself plenty of time to get there. Plan to arrive somewhat ahead of the scheduled time, particularly if your appointment is in the fore part of the day. If a previous candidate fails to appear, the board might be ready for you a bit early. By early afternoon an oral board is almost invariably behind schedule if there are many candidates, and you may have to wait. Take along a book or magazine to read, or your application to review, but leave any extraneous material in the waiting room when you go in for your interview. In any event, relax and compose yourself.

The matter of dress is important. The board is forming impressions about you – from your experience, your manners, your attitude, and your appearance. Give your personal appearance careful attention. Dress your best, but not your flashiest. Choose conservative, appropriate clothing, and be sure it is immaculate. This is a business interview, and your appearance should indicate that you regard it as such. Besides, being well groomed and properly dressed will help boost your confidence.

Sooner or later, someone will call your name and escort you into the interview room. *This is it.* From here on you are on your own. It is too late for any more preparation. But remember, you asked for this opportunity to prove your fitness, and you are here because your request was granted.

What happens when you go in?

The usual sequence of events will be as follows: The clerk (who is often the board stenographer) will introduce you to the chairman of the oral board, who will introduce you to the other members of the board. Acknowledge the introductions before you sit down. Do not be surprised if you find a microphone facing you or a stenotypist sitting by. Oral interviews are usually recorded in the event of an appeal or other review.

Usually the chairman of the board will open the interview by reviewing the highlights of your education and work experience from your application – primarily for the benefit of the other members of the board, as well as to get the material into the record. Do not interrupt or comment unless there is an error or significant misinterpretation; if that is the case, do not hesitate. But do not quibble about insignificant matters. Also, he will usually ask you some question about your education, experience or your present job – partly to get you to start talking and to establish the interviewing "rapport." He may start the actual questioning, or turn it over to one of the other members. Frequently, each member undertakes the questioning on a particular area, one in which he is perhaps most competent, so you can expect each member to participate in the examination. Because time is limited, you may also expect some rather abrupt switches in the direction the questioning takes, so do not be upset by it. Normally, a board member will not pursue a single line of questioning unless he discovers a particular strength or weakness.

After each member has participated, the chairman will usually ask whether any member has any further questions, then will ask you if you have anything you wish to add. Unless you are expecting this question, it may floor you. Worse, it may start you off on an extended, extemporaneous speech. The board is not usually seeking more information. The question is principally to offer you a last opportunity to present further qualifications or to indicate that you have nothing to add. So, if you feel that a significant qualification or characteristic has been overlooked, it is proper to point it out in a sentence or so. Do not compliment the board on the thoroughness of their examination – they have been sketchy, and you know it. If you wish, merely say, "No thank you, I have nothing further to add." This is a point where you can "talk yourself out" of a good impression or fail to present an important bit of information. Remember, *you close the interview yourself*.

The chairman will then say, "That is all, Mr. _____, thank you." Do not be startled; the interview is over, and quicker than you think. Thank him, gather your belongings and take your leave. Save your sigh of relief for the other side of the door.

How to put your best foot forward

Throughout this entire process, you may feel that the board individually and collectively is trying to pierce your defenses, seek out your hidden weaknesses and embarrass and confuse you. Actually, this is not true. They are obliged to make an appraisal of your qualifications for the job you are seeking, and they want to see you in your best light. Remember, they must interview all candidates and a non-cooperative candidate may become a failure in spite of their best efforts to bring out his qualifications. Here are 15 suggestions that will help you:

1) Be natural – Keep your attitude confident, not cocky

If you are not confident that you can do the job, do not expect the board to be. Do not apologize for your weaknesses, try to bring out your strong points. The board is interested in a positive, not negative, presentation. Cockiness will antagonize any board member and make him wonder if you are covering up a weakness by a false show of strength.

2) Get comfortable, but don't lounge or sprawl

Sit erectly but not stiffly. A careless posture may lead the board to conclude that you are careless in other things, or at least that you are not impressed by the importance of the occasion. Either conclusion is natural, even if incorrect. Do not fuss with your clothing, a pencil or an ashtray. Your hands may occasionally be useful to emphasize a point; do not let them become a point of distraction.

3) Do not wisecrack or make small talk

This is a serious situation, and your attitude should show that you consider it as such. Further, the time of the board is limited – they do not want to waste it, and neither should you.

4) Do not exaggerate your experience or abilities
In the first place, from information in the application or other interviews and sources, the board may know more about you than you think. Secondly, you probably will not get away with it. An experienced board is rather adept at spotting such a situation, so do not take the chance.

5) If you know a board member, do not make a point of it, yet do not hide it
Certainly you are not fooling him, and probably not the other members of the board. Do not try to take advantage of your acquaintanceship – it will probably do you little good.

6) Do not dominate the interview
Let the board do that. They will give you the clues – do not assume that you have to do all the talking. Realize that the board has a number of questions to ask you, and do not try to take up all the interview time by showing off your extensive knowledge of the answer to the first one.

7) Be attentive
You only have 20 minutes or so, and you should keep your attention at its sharpest throughout. When a member is addressing a problem or question to you, give him your undivided attention. Address your reply principally to him, but do not exclude the other board members.

8) Do not interrupt
A board member may be stating a problem for you to analyze. He will ask you a question when the time comes. Let him state the problem, and wait for the question.

9) Make sure you understand the question
Do not try to answer until you are sure what the question is. If it is not clear, restate it in your own words or ask the board member to clarify it for you. However, do not haggle about minor elements.

10) Reply promptly but not hastily
A common entry on oral board rating sheets is "candidate responded readily," or "candidate hesitated in replies." Respond as promptly and quickly as you can, but do not jump to a hasty, ill-considered answer.

11) Do not be peremptory in your answers
A brief answer is proper – but do not fire your answer back. That is a losing game from your point of view. The board member can probably ask questions much faster than you can answer them.

12) Do not try to create the answer you think the board member wants
He is interested in what kind of mind you have and how it works – not in playing games. Furthermore, he can usually spot this practice and will actually grade you down on it.

13) Do not switch sides in your reply merely to agree with a board member
Frequently, a member will take a contrary position merely to draw you out and to see if you are willing and able to defend your point of view. Do not start a debate, yet do not surrender a good position. If a position is worth taking, it is worth defending.

14) Do not be afraid to admit an error in judgment if you are shown to be wrong

The board knows that you are forced to reply without any opportunity for careful consideration. Your answer may be demonstrably wrong. If so, admit it and get on with the interview.

15) Do not dwell at length on your present job

The opening question may relate to your present assignment. Answer the question but do not go into an extended discussion. You are being examined for a *new* job, not your present one. As a matter of fact, try to phrase ALL your answers in terms of the job for which you are being examined.

Basis of Rating

Probably you will forget most of these "do's" and "don'ts" when you walk into the oral interview room. Even remembering them all will not ensure you a passing grade. Perhaps you did not have the qualifications in the first place. But remembering them will help you to put your best foot forward, without treading on the toes of the board members.

Rumor and popular opinion to the contrary notwithstanding, an oral board wants you to make the best appearance possible. They know you are under pressure – but they also want to see how you respond to it as a guide to what your reaction would be under the pressures of the job you seek. They will be influenced by the degree of poise you display, the personal traits you show and the manner in which you respond.

ABOUT THIS BOOK

This book contains tests divided into Examination Sections. Go through each test, answering every question in the margin. We have also attached a sample answer sheet at the back of the book that can be removed and used. At the end of each test look at the answer key and check your answers. On the ones you got wrong, look at the right answer choice and learn. Do not fill in the answers first. Do not memorize the questions and answers, but understand the answer and principles involved. On your test, the questions will likely be different from the samples. Questions are changed and new ones added. If you understand these past questions you should have success with any changes that arise. Tests may consist of several types of questions. We have additional books on each subject should more study be advisable or necessary for you. Finally, the more you study, the better prepared you will be. This book is intended to be the last thing you study before you walk into the examination room. Prior study of relevant texts is also recommended. NLC publishes some of these in our Fundamental Series. Knowledge and good sense are important factors in passing your exam. Good luck also helps. So now study this Passbook, absorb the material contained within and take that knowledge into the examination. Then do your best to pass that exam.

EXAMINATION SECTION

EXAMINATION SECTION
TEST 1

DIRECTIONS: Each question or incomplete statement is followed by several suggested answers or completions. Select the one that BEST answers the question or completes the statement. *PRINT THE LETTER OF THE CORRECT ANSWER IN THE SPACE AT THE RIGHT.*

1. Normal reflexes during the neonatal period include

   A. moro
   B. grasp
   C. stepping
   D. all of the above

   1._____

2. The milestone MOST likely to occur at 12 weeks of age is the infant's

   A. sustaining social contact
   B. laughing out loud
   C. rolling over
   D. sitting with pelvic support

   2._____

3. A newborn infant CANNOT

   A. turn his head
   B. touch a surface with his nose
   C. lift his head to the plane of the body
   D. flex around his supporting hand

   3._____

4. The age at which an infant starts to sustain his head in the plane of the body is APPROXIMATELY _____ month(s).

   A. one
   B. two
   C. three
   D. four

   4._____

5. At 4 months of age, an infant can do all of the following EXCEPT

   A. sit with a truncal support
   B. show displeasure if social contact is broken
   C. roll over
   D. none of the above

   5._____

6. An infant starts using pincer movement at APPROXIMATELY _____ of age.

   A. five
   B. six
   C. eight
   D. nine

   6._____

7. At what age can a child imitate a number or letter figure? _____ months.

   A. 18
   B. 30
   C. 36
   D. None of the above

   7._____

8. Which of the following is a cognitive milestone achieved by a child at 28 weeks?

   A. Releasing one cube into a cup after demonstration
   B. Raking at a pallet
   C. Uncovering a hidden object
   D. Knowing one or more words and their meanings

   8._____

9. A 3-month-old infant can do all of the following EXCEPT

   A. listen to music
   B. creep-crawl
   C. fail to grasp
   D. sustain social contact

   9._____

1

10. Unassisted pincer movement develops at the age of _____ months.

    A. four   B. six   C. eight   D. twelve

11. At 6 months of age, developmental milestones do NOT include the child's

    A. putting a pellet into a bottle
    B. releasing two cubes into a cup
    C. scribbling spontaneously
    D. enjoying a simple ball game

12. Which of the following is NOT a normal accomplishment of a child at 18 months of age?

    A. Learning to say *no*
    B. Listening to stories while looking at the pictures
    C. Identifying one or more body parts
    D. Kissing parent with a pucker

13. Normal milestones at 2 months of age include the infant's doing each of the following EXCEPT

    A. reaching at objects
    B. smiling on social contact
    C. attending to voices and coos
    D. following a moving object to 180 visually

14. A 15-month-old child can do all of the following EXCEPT

    A. walk alone
    B. crawl up stairs
    C. imitate a stroke of crayon
    D. make a tower of 3 cubes

15. During the second year of life, weight gain averages _____ kg per year.

    A. 1   B. 2.5   C. 3.5   D. 5

16. During the second year of life, height gain averages APPROXIMATELY _____ centimeters per year.

    A. 2   B. 6   C. 10   D. 15

17. At what age does a child usually reach double the length of his birth length? _____ year(s).

    A. 1   B. 2   C. 3   D. 4

18. A 15-month-old child can make a tower of _____ cubes.

    A. 3   B. 5   C. 7   D. 9

19. A 4-year-old child generally CANNOT

    A. throw a ball   B. climb well
    C. copy a triangle   D. hop on one foot

20. Which of the following is NOT considered a normal motor milestone for a child 3 years of age?

    A. Building a 10-cube tower
    B. Copying a circle
    C. Copying a square
    D. Attempting to draw a person

21. A normally developing 2-year-old child can do all of the following EXCEPT

    A. handle a spoon well
    B. alternate feet while going upstairs
    C. fold paper imitatively
    D. climb on furniture

22. At what age can a child with normal social and cognitive development know his or her own age and sex?
    At _____ months of age.

    A. 18   B. 24   C. 30   D. 36

23. A 3-year-old child can do all of the following EXCEPT

    A. alternate feet while going downstairs
    B. ride a tricycle
    C. hop on one foot
    D. repeat three numbers

24. Nuts, pitted fruits, and popcorn should not be given to a toddler PRIMARILY because they

    A. have almost no food value for a toddler
    B. can cause tooth cavities
    C. will affect the child's appetite
    D. are easily aspirated

25. All of the following statements describe toddlers' well-known sleeping patterns EXCEPT:

    A. Toddlers' sleep needs average 12 hours per day.
    B. A toddler typically discontinues daytime naps around age 3.
    C. A toddler typically sleeps through the night and has at least three daytime naps.
    D. A consistent bedtime ritual helps prepare a toddler for sleep.

26. The one of the following immunizations that is NOT necessary for a toddler to receive is

    A. MMR (measles, mumps, and rubella)
    B. DPT-4, OPV-3 (if not given earlier), PRP-D
    C. HBPV (hemophilus influenzae type B polysaccharide vaccine)
    D. DPT-5, OPV-4

27. Which of the following statements about toddlers' physical growth and development is NOT correct?

    A. Bow-leggedness typically persists through toddlerhood since the legs must bear the weight of the relatively large trunk.
    B. Growth of about 3 inches per year and an average height of 34 inches at age 2 years is normal for toddlers.
    C. Gain of about 4 to 6 lbs. per year and an average weight of 27 lbs. at age 2 years is normal for toddlers.
    D. In toddlers, height and weight increase in a linear fashion.

28. All of the following information about toddlers' psycho-motor milestones is correct EXCEPT:

    A. Sensory changes increase as proximodistal sensations heighten.
    B. The toddler typically begins to walk by age 12 to 15 months, to run by age 2 years, and to walk backward and hop on one foot by age 3 years.
    C. By 24 months of age, a toddler usually achieves fairly good bowel and bladder control.
    D. The toddler usually cannot alternate feet when climbing stairs.

29. All of the following describe normal height and weight changes in children of 3 to 6 years of age EXCEPT:

    A. Gain of 6 to 8 lbs. per year
    B. Average height of 37 inches at age 3, 40 1/2 inches at age 4, and 43 inches at age 5
    C. Growth of 2 1/2 to 3 inches per year
    D. Average weight of 32 lbs. at age 3, 37 lbs. at age 4, and 41 lbs. at age 5

30. Which of the following is NOT a true fact about psycho-motor milestones of children age 3 to 6 years?
A preschooler

    A. demonstrates increased skill in balancing; by age 4 or 5, he or she can balance on alternate feet with eyes closed
    B. alternates feet when climbing stairs, indicating increased balance and coordination
    C. can successfully perform jobs such as using scissors
    D. is still not skilled enough to tie his or her shoelaces

KEY (CORRECT ANSWERS)

1. D
2. A
3. C
4. B
5. C

6. D
7. C
8. B
9. B
10. D

11. C
12. B
13. A
14. C
15. B

16. B
17. D
18. A
19. C
20. C

21. B
22. D
23. C
24. D
25. C

26. D
27. D
28. C
29. A
30. D

TEST 2

DIRECTIONS: Each question or incomplete statement is followed by several suggested answers or completions. Select the one that BEST answers the question or completes the statement. *PRINT THE LETTER OF THE CORRECT ANSWER IN THE SPACE AT THE RIGHT.*

1. Toys play a useful role in a child's development. All of the following factors should be taken into consideration while selecting a toy for a toddler EXCEPT 1.____

   A. expense
   B. durability
   C. safety
   D. weight

2. All of the following are appropriate and important components for disciplining a toddler EXCEPT 2.____

   A. distraction
   B. admonishment
   C. explanation
   D. praise

3. Which of the following statements MOST accurately describes the toilet training of a toddler? 3.____

   A. Bowel control is accomplished by 18 months.
   B. Daytime bladder control is achieved by 12 to 24 months.
   C. Nightime bladder control is achieved by 24 to 36 months.
   D. Toilet training is usually completed by 4 1/2 years.

4. A toddler's daily nutritional needs from the four basic food groups do NOT include 4.____

   A. two servings from the meat group, 2 tablespoons per serving
   B. four servings from the fruit and vegetable group, 2 tablespoons per serving
   C. seven or more servings of breads and cereals, 1 slice of bread or 3/4 to 1 cup of cereal per serving
   D. 3 cups of milk or milk products

5. John and Peter, both 3 years of age, are fighting over a toy train. 5.____
   Which of the following interventions would be the MOST appropriate in this situation?

   A. Admonish them for fighting and tell them to share the train.
   B. Tell them to stop fighting and that there are enough toys to play with, and give Peter puzzles.
   C. Without saying anything, take the train away from the boys and place them in separate parts of the room, giving them some other toys to play with.
   D. Find another train and tell them that they can each have one.

6. Which of the following characteristics is NOT typical of a toddler's language development? 6.____

   A. Begins to use short sentences at 18 months to 2 years
   B. Can remember and repeat 3 numbers by 3 years
   C. Answers questions with multi-word sentences
   D. After knowing own name by 12 months, gives first name by 24 months and full name by 3 years

7. A child commonly experiences more fears during the preschool period than at any other time.
   All of the following are good examples of preschoolers' common fears EXCEPT

   A. being left alone
   B. body mutilation
   C. small animals like rabbits, cats, etc.
   D. objects associated with painful experiences

8. In a conflict situation among preschoolers, which of the following disciplinary principles would be considered the BEST nursing intervention to help the child relieve intensity, regain control, and think about his or her behavior?

   A. Explaining to the child the negative aspects of the conflict
   B. Admonishing the child for the conflict
   C. Distracting the child by providing him with one of the toys he or she likes most
   D. Giving the child a short time-out of 1 minute per year of age

9. All of the following are findings of Freud's theory of psychosexual development of toddlers EXCEPT:

   A. The toddler experiences nothing else but a deep frustration as he or she gains control over containing and releasing bodily waste.
   B. In this stage, the child's focus shifts from the mouth to the anal area, with emphasis on bowel control as he or she gains neuromuscular control over the anal sphincter.
   C. In the *anal stage,* typically extending from age 8 months to 4 years, the erogenous zone is the anus and buttocks, and sexual activity centers on expulsion and retention of bodily waste.
   D. The conflict between *holding on* and *letting go* gradually resolves as bowel training progresses; resolution occurs once control is firmly established.

10. It is NOT true that a toddler of age 15 to 18 months

    A. does not have any signs of temper tantrums yet
    B. walks sideways and backwards
    C. imitates simple things
    D. pulls a toy while walking

11. Which of the following statements about toddlers' play activities is NOT correct?

    A. For a toddler, play is a major socializing medium.
    B. Play typically is parallel - beside rather than with another child.
    C. Push-pull toys help enhance walking skills.
    D. Because of a toddler's long attention span, he or she does not change toys often.

12. Of the following, the INCORRECT statement about toddlers' language and socialization patterns is:

    A. A toddler tends to ask many *what* questions
    B. A toddler typically begins to use longer sentences and has a vocabulary of about 500 words by age 2
    C. A toddler's social interaction is dominated by ritualism, negativism, and independence

D. Confidence in separating from parents continues to grow

13. Common fears of toddlers include all of the following EXCEPT   13.____

    A. loss of parents, separation anxiety
    B. stranger anxiety
    C. musical toys' noises
    D. large animals

14. Discipline strategies are affected by a toddler's temperament.   14.____
    Which of the following disciplinary approaches would likely be the MOST effective for a *difficult* child?

    A. Sustained eye contact and a stern voice
    B. A friendly warning to curtail activities with structured time-out if necessary
    C. Time for gradual introduction to new situations
    D. A quick spanking with explanation for misbehavior

15. The toddler's feeling that commonly develops after a new baby is born, stemming from a   15.____
    sense of *dethronement* since he or she no longer is the sole focus of his parent's attention, is known as

    A. identification   B. mitleiden
    C. sibling rivalry   D. motivation

16. All of the following are considered as important interventions to prevent injuries in toddlers EXCEPT: 16.____

    A. Instruct parents to keep crib rails up, place gates across stairways, keep screens secure on all windows, and supervise the toddler at play
    B. Instruct parents never to forget about tightening the car safety belt while riding a toddler around in a car
    C. Teach parents to place all toxic substances up high and locked; secure safety caps on medications; and remove all small, easily aspirated objects from the child's environment
    D. Instruct parents to avoid using table covers to prevent spilling of hot foods or liquids by the child on himself or herself

17. Which of the following statements is NOT part of Piaget's Theory of Cognitive Development of toddlers?   17.____

    A. The theory is expressed in two phases, i.e., the Sensorimotor phase and the Preconceptual phase.
    B. The first stage of the Sensorimotor phase explains the primary circular reactions at the age of 12 to 14 months.
    C. The second stage of the Sensorimotor phase explains the beginning of thought at the age of 18 to 24 months, during which time the toddler begins to devise new means for accomplishing tasks through mental calculations.
    D. In the Preconceptual phase, extending from about age 2 to 4 years, the child uses representational thought to recall the past, represent the present, and anticipate the future.

18. According to Kohlberg's Theory of Moral Development of toddlers, moral judgment is a cognitive process that develops gradually at all of these levels EXCEPT the _____ level.   18.____

    A. paraconventional   B. preconventional
    C. conventional   D. postconventional

19. The Denver Developmental Screening Test (DDST) evaluates a child's _____ development.   19.____

    A. social   B. motor
    C. physical   D. all of the above

20. According to Erikson's theory of psychosocial development, the toddler begins to master all of the following EXCEPT   20.____

    A. individuation
    B. control of bodily functions
    C. control of the sense of autonomy, and moves on to master the task of initiative
    D. acquisition of socially acceptable behavior

21. Kohlberg's Theory of Moral Development for preschoolers does NOT include the finding that   21.____

    A. a preschooler is in the preconventional phase of moral development, which extends from 5 to 8 years of age
    B. in this phase, conscience emerges and the emphasis is on external control
    C. a preschooler's preconventional phase of moral development extends from age 4 to 10 years
    D. a preschooler's moral standards are those of others, and he or she observes them either to avoid punishment or to reap rewards

22. Which of the following statements is FALSE concerning the language skills of a preschooler?   22.____

    A. A preschooler's vocabulary typically increases to about 1300 words by age 3.
    B. By age 5, a preschooler's vocabulary typically increases to about 2100 words.
    C. A preschooler may talk incessantly and ask many *why* questions.
    D. By age 3, a child usually talks in three- or four-word sentences.

23. Which of the following is considered MOST appropriate to aid gross motor development of a preschooler?   23.____

    A. Dress-up clothes
    B. Paints, paper, and crayons
    C. Swimming
    D. Field trips to museums and parks

24. A preschooler needs regular interaction with agemates to help develop _____ skills.   24.____

    A. creative   B. imaginative   C. motor   D. social

25. According to Erikson's Theory of Psychosocial Development, between 3 and 6 years of age, a child faces a psycho-social crisis which Erikson terms _____ vs. _____ .   25.____

    A. definitive; initiative   B. initiative; terminative
    C. terminative; fear   D. initiative; guilt

26. According to Erikson's Theory, the development of a sense of guilt occurs when the child is made to feel that his or her imagination and activities are unacceptable.
Guilt, anxiety, and fear result when the child's thoughts and actions clash with parents'

   A. guilt
   B. fear
   C. anxiety
   D. expectations

26._____

27. Freud terms his Theory of Psychosexual Development of Preschoolers all of the following EXCEPT the _____ stage.

   A. phallic
   B. oedipal
   C. oediphallic
   D. all of the above

27._____

28. In the phallic stage of Freud's theory, extending from about age 3 to 7, the child's pleasure centers on

   A. the attention given by the parents
   B. friendship with children of the opposite sex
   C. genitalia and masturbation
   D. all of the above

28._____

29. Piaget, who defines his Theory of Cognitive Development for preschoolers as a stage of preconceptual thoughts, classifies his theory in two phases, i.e., preconceptual phase and intuitive phase.
He includes all of the following activities in the preconceptual phase, which extends from age 2 to 4, EXCEPT

   A. making simple classifications
   B. reasoning from specific to specific
   C. exhibiting egocentric thinking
   D. forming concepts that are complete and logical

29._____

30. According to the intuitive phase of Piaget's theory, which extends from age 4 to 7, it is NOT correct that a preschooler

   A. becomes capable of classifying, quantifying, and relating objects
   B. exhibits intuitive thought processes
   C. is aware of the principles behind classifying and relating objects
   D. uses many words appropriately but without a real knowledge of their meaning

30._____

KEY (CORRECT ANSWERS)

1.	A	16.	B
2.	B	17.	B
3.	A	18.	A
4.	C	19.	D
5.	D	20.	C
6.	C	21.	A
7.	C	22.	A
8.	D	23.	C
9.	A	24.	D
10.	A	25.	D
11.	D	26.	D
12.	B	27.	C
13.	C	28.	C
14.	B	29.	D
15.	C	30.	C

EXAMINATION SECTION
TEST 1

DIRECTIONS: Each question or incomplete statement is followed by several suggested answers or completions. Select the one that BEST answers the question or completes the statement. *PRINT THE LETTER OF THE CORRECT ANSWER IN THE SPACE AT THE RIGHT.*

1. Which one of the following statements is TRUE with respect to the development of language ability? 1._____

    A. Boys tend to talk a little earlier than girls.
    B. Twins tend to talk earlier than single children.
    C. The amount of stimulation in the home environment is a relatively unimportant factor in the development of language.
    D. Children who talk earliest generally prove to be most intelligent when tested at a later age.

2. Which of the following statements is LEAST likely to be TRUE of first-grade children as compared with fifth graders? 2._____

    A. There is much concern for group welfare and group approval.
    B. There is little concern for order and neatness.
    C. Some regular routines give security to children of this age.
    D. There is little intermingling of boys and girls in their play activities.

3. Reasoning begins to develop in children during the period of the _____ years. 3._____

    A. pre-school
    B. primary school
    C. intermediate school
    D. high school

4. Growth 4._____

    A. is saltatory
    B. proceeds most rapidly during the adolescent years
    C. follows an orderly genetic sequence in the emergence of behavior patterns
    D. depends entirely on maturation

5. When the individual perceives relationships, observes which things belong together, and which things do not, or observes the relation between means and ends, he is said to 5._____

    A. introspect
    B. remember
    C. learn by "insight"
    D. possess eidetic imagery

6. Investigators have found a small but consistent superiority of females over males in _____ ability. 6._____

    A. artistic
    B. linguistic
    C. arithmetical
    D. reasoning

7. Mental development and physical development are _____ correlated. 7._____

    A. highly
    B. perfectly
    C. only very slightly
    D. not in the least

8. Which of the following statements is MOST in agreement with modern theories of child development? Growth is a(n)

   A. continuous process, uniform in rate
   B. continuous process, but it is not uniform in rate
   C. predictable process, but so highly individual that group generalizations should not be attempted
   D. unpredictable process in which patterns are difficult to establish

9. Generally, which of the following influences exerts the GREATEST impact on the development of the self-concept in fifteen-year-old individuals?

   A. Acceptance by their friends and classmates
   B. Acceptance by their teachers
   C. Ideals and aspirations
   D. Knowledge of their abilities from school experiences

10. In comparing boys and girls as to the period of peak body growth, called the "prepuberal growth spurt," it can be said that, on the average,

    A. girls precede boys by about eighteen months
    B. the phenomenon occurs in both sexes at about the same time
    C. boys precede girls by about one year
    D. girls precede boys by about six months

11. As a child grows older, outwardly visible signs of emotion become

    A. more intense   B. more common
    C. less frequent   D. less important

12. Fairy tales are MOST popular with children whose age is

    A. 3 years   B. 5 years
    C. 7 years   D. 9 years

13. Of the following, the MOST suitable active game for seven-year-old children is

    A. London Bridge   B. Looby-Loo
    C. dodge ball   D. Cobbler, Mend My Shoe

14. All of the following are characteristic of the typical four-year-old EXCEPT

    A. his attention span is short
    B. his coordination is not well-developed
    C. he is not likely to be interested in people
    D. he is not likely to share things with other children

15. Of the following physical characteristics of the pre-kindergarten child, the one which is INCORRECT is that he

    A. begins to develop small muscle control
    B. is susceptible to communicable diseases
    C. is usually near-sighted
    D. needs frequent rest

16. Of the following, the GREATEST factor in the motor development of a five-year-old child is

    A. steady practice
    B. mental ability
    C. maturation
    D. home environment

17. Of the following, the statement which BEST describes the child of kindergarten age is that he

    A. is adept at projecting himself into other places and times
    B. is incapable of any flights of imagination
    C. seldom questions anything in his physical environment
    D. is bound to the here and now by his stage of organic development, as well as by his limited experience

18. Of the following, the PRIME reason why five-year-olds are often willing to share their things is that they

    A. seek adult approval
    B. have no interest in possessions
    C. have no use for them
    D. prefer companions to possessions

19. Research tends to show that all of the following are TRUE of development of language in children of pre-school and elementary school age EXCEPT that

    A. girls tend to be poorer than boys in clarity of enunciation and freedom from speech defects
    B. the number of basic words known increases by several thousands per year
    C. the length of responses tends to increase with the age of the child
    D. the average length of sentences spoken by girls is greater than it is for boys of the same age

20. Of the following, the natural sequence of language growth is

    A. listening, reading, speaking, writing
    B. reading, listening, speaking, writing
    C. listening, speaking, reading, writing
    D. listening, speaking, writing, reading

21. Of the following parts of speech, the one which predominates in the vocabulary of a child beginning to speak is

    A. adjectives
    B. nouns
    C. verbs
    D. pronouns

22. All of the following are known for writings in the area of child growth and development EXCEPT

    A. Frances Ilg
    B. Anna B. Comstock
    C. Arnold Gesell
    D. Maria Montessori

23. All of the following are characteristic of the average seven-year-old EXCEPT that he

    A. likes to bat and pitch a ball
    B. fits easily into organized group play

C. enjoys alternate periods of activity and inactivity
D. shows more interest in some activities and tries fewer new ventures than the four-year-old

24. All of the following statements regarding language arts in early childhood education are true EXCEPT

   A. if a number of children wander away while the teacher is reading a story, it may be that they have had too many sedentary activities that day
   B. storytelling - as opposed to story reading - should be undertaken only when the teacher feels she is unable to read the story with sufficient dramatic expression to maintain the children's interest
   C. listening to rhythmic poetry affords much enjoyment to young children
   D. the line between fantasy and reality is generally not sharply defined in the mind of the four-year-old child

25. All of the following statements concerning social relationships in the early school years are usually true EXCEPT

   A. groups are small and shift rapidly
   B. friends are selected because of propinquity and the accident of sharing objects
   C. children play and work with others to satisfy personal rather than social desires
   D. friends are selected on the basis of belonging to the same sex

26. In general, the language development of girls is

   A. more rapid than that of boys
   B. less rapid than that of boys
   C. equal to that of boys
   D. more rapid than that of boys in oral communication, but slower in written communication

27. Defense mechanisms are used

   A. *most frequently* by average children
   B. *less frequently* by slow learners than by average children
   C. *more frequently* by slow learners than by average children
   D. *by all children* regardless of level of ability

28. Research in child development shows that all children have

   A. a single, fixed design of growth
   B. individual potentialities for various patterns of growth
   C. equal abilities for growth in all areas
   D. no consistent growth patterns

29. The period designated as "early childhood"

   A. is a period when memory is high
   B. is a time of very rapid growth
   C. is relatively unimportant so far as learning is concerned
   D. is a time when there is little change in physical structure

30. Of the following, the one MOST characteristic of the normally developing adolescent is   30._____

    A. continuous need for parental support
    B. development of emotional maturity
    C. desire for constant domination by siblings
    D. freedom from peer group identification

31. The normal child on entering school knows the meaning of about   31._____

    A. 500 words   B. 1,000 words
    C. 2,000 words   D. 3,000 words

32. For a four-year-old child, the events of the present are   32._____

    A. less vivid than those of the past
    B. less vivid than those of the future
    C. more vivid than those of the past or future
    D. as vivid as those of the past or future

33. The EARLIEST aesthetic experiences of the young child are likely to occur in play with   33._____

    A. blocks and paints
    B. games and toys
    C. swings, see-saws, and sliding ponds
    D. kitchen and household utensils

34. Of the following characteristics of child development, the one MOST closely related to the 10-12 age group is   34._____

    A. difficulty with gross motor coordination
    B. eagerness for peer approval
    C. anxiety to please the teacher
    D. interest in the immediate environment

35. The one of the following which is a psychological principle which can BEST be described as a situation in which an individual experiences some ambivalence and indecisiveness in choosing one or more desired objects or goals is   35._____

    A. task-orientation   B. conflict
    C. apathy   D. projection

36. The treatment method which allows or encourages the client to express his charged feelings around a pressing emotional need is known as   36._____

    A. exploring   B. synthesizing
    C. catharsis   D. ventilating

37. The emotional release that results from recall of a previously forgotten painful experience is known as   37._____

    A. introjection   B. abreaction
    C. sublimation   D. free association

38. The action whereby an individual directs his aggression against an innocent bystander rather than expressing it against the source of his difficulties is called

    A. displacement
    B. projection
    C. introjection
    D. abreaction

39. An attempt to attribute emotionally caused behavior to reasonable factors MORE acceptable to the individual is known as

    A. projection
    B. rationalization
    C. introjection
    D. free association

40. The unconscious application of elements of the experiences in a former relationship to a new relationship is known as

    A. projection
    B. abreaction
    C. transference
    D. sublimation

41. In reference to learning, most children will tend to set goals for themselves which are

    A. similar to those of their peers
    B. different from those of their peers
    C. too difficult or complex
    D. too easy or too low

42. Children involved in initial learning tend to do significantly better on problems where the rule or principle is

    A. given or stated
    B. independently derived
    C. minimized
    D. neglected

43. Studies of sensory deprivation during infancy indicate that lack of stimulation during this period is most likely to result in

    A. low frustration tolerance
    B. poor psychomotor coordination
    C. lack of emotional responsiveness
    D. delayed intellectual development

44. When do coordination and convergence of the eyes begin to develop in the infant?

    A. Immediately after birth
    B. After one week
    C. After two weeks
    D. After three weeks

45. In the IOWA studies of children's reactions to frustration, which one of the following reactions was LEAST observed?

    A. Regression
    B. Aggression
    C. Resignation
    D. Accommodation

46. Dick, who is 14 years old, has been given a curfew of midnight. Arriving home at 2:30 A.M., he explains his decision to come in late was based on the fact that everyone his age stays out that late. He is using

    A. compensation
    B. denial
    C. displacement
    D. rationalization

47. By virtue of his earlier interaction with his mother, a child may display affectional responses to other adults.
This is an example of

   A. secondary reinforcement
   B. stimulus generalization
   C. response diffusion
   D. learned mediation

   47._____

48. Which one of the following BEST illustrates the distinction between "performance" and "competence" as drawn by contemporary psycholinguists?

   A. A child can vocalize before he can speak.
   B. A child's motor development depends upon language acquisition.
   C. A child is more limited in language production than in language comprehension.
   D. A child acquires language to meet his need to function as an effective person.

   48._____

49. Bruner and Page, among others, contend that children can learn anything that adults can. Ausubel, in his writings,

   A. extends the contention
   B. modifies the contention
   C. rejects the contention
   D. supports the contention

   49._____

50. An 8-year-old pupil is told by his teacher that he cannot join his group in play because he needs to practice writing. The boy starts crying, drops to the floor, sobs heavily and strikes the floor with hands and legs. The behavior exhibited by the boy is an example of

   A. repression
   B. identification
   C. aggression
   D. regression

   50._____

KEY (CORRECT ANSWERS)

1.	D	11.	C	21.	B	31.	B	41.	A
2.	A	12.	C	22.	B	32.	C	42.	A
3.	A	13.	C	23.	B	33.	A	43.	D
4.	C	14.	C	24.	B	34.	B	44.	A
5.	C	15.	C	25.	A	35.	B	45.	D
6.	B	16.	C	26.	A	36.	D	46.	D
7.	C	17.	D	27.	D	37.	B	47.	B
8.	B	18.	A	28.	B	38.	A	48.	C
9.	A	19.	A	29.	B	39.	B	49.	C
10.	A	20.	C	30.	B	40.	C	50.	D

EXAMINATION SECTION
TEST 1

DIRECTIONS: Each question or incomplete statement is followed by several suggested answers or completions. Select the one that BEST answers the question or completes the statement. *PRINT THE LETTER OF THE CORRECT ANSWER IN THE SPACE AT THE RIGHT.*

1. Of the following, the area of greatest similarity among children is in their

    A. inherited traits
    B. rates of development
    C. sequences of development
    D. patterns of growth dimensions
    E. perceptual and conceptual development

2. Of the following, which is the MOST significant factor in determining the choice of friends among children between the ages of six and ten?

    A. Mutual interests
    B. Similar personality traits
    C. Conveniently close location
    D. Social and economic standing of parents
    E. Physical maturity

3. Joe Flirp is a great health education teacher, to a large extent, because the boys model themselves after him. The foregoing illustrates the psychological mechanism of

    A. sublimation
    B. displacement
    C. regression
    D. identification
    E. projection

4. "You're much too authoritarian," said the principal to the teacher. "And I won't stand for that in my school." The principal is demonstrating the psychological mechanism of

    A. sublimation
    B. conversion
    C. projection
    D. identification
    E. displaced aggression

5. Margaret Snorble, unhappy because of her lack of friendship, devoted all her energy to studying. She became the number one student in her grade. Margaret is demonstrating the psychological mechanism of

    A. sublimation
    B. conversion
    C. introjection
    D. fantasy
    E. rationalization

6. Joanie asked for apple pie and was told that there was none left. "Oh well," said she, "give me peach pie. I like it better anyway." Joanie is demonstrating the psychological mechanism of

    A. regression
    B. displacement
    C. rationalization
    D. sublimation
    E. recidivism

7. The principal had just left after telling Miss Jones she had to improve the quality of her lesson plans. Tears came to her eyes; she stamped her foot several times, pounded on the desk and then broke into uncontrolled sobbing. Miss Jones' behavior is an example of the psychological mechanism of

   A. introjection
   B. projection
   C. sublimation
   D. regression
   E. displaced hostility

8. Of the following statements concerning praise and punishment, which is LEAST in accord with modern psychological principles?

   A. When a child is bad, spank him.
   B. When a child is bad, say, "If you're not good, I won't love you any more."
   C. When a child is good, give him something to show your approval.
   D. When a child is good, say, "That's O.K. Let's try to do better next time."
   E. When a child is good, do not over-reinforce him.

9. Defining personality as the end-product of our habit systems expresses a concept most characteristic of a psychological orientation termed

   A. behavioristic
   B. psychoanalytic
   C. Gestalt
   D. personalistic
   E. structuralistic

10. Studies on intelligence and creativity have yielded findings which indicate that

    A. the two characteristics are completely independent
    B. they are independent for subjects of high average ability and above
    C. they are negatively correlated
    D. for all practical purposes, measuring one trait is essentially the same as measuring the other
    E. the two characteristics vary in pattern, depending on the particular individual being tested

11. A five-year-old is walking with his father and notes that there is a full moon. He says, "Daddy, the moon is following us." What type of thinking is exemplified by the child's comment?

    A. Syncretism
    B. Centralism
    C. Autism
    D. Primatism
    E. Egocentrism

12. The process whereby an individual develops great sympathy towards another in order to conceal from himself certain malicious feelings toward this person, is known as

    A. rationalization
    B. intropunitiveness
    C. extrapunitiveness
    D. reaction formation
    E. introjection

13. Paranoia is best understood in terms of the mechanism of

    A. projection
    B. regression
    C. hostility
    D. reaction formation
    E. sublimation

14. The MOST practicable procedure yet found to identify persons who are not giving honest answers in a personality inventory is to

    A. include a set of items which sound good but which few honest persons would answer in the "good" direction
    B. repeat the inventory at a later date
    C. check the consistency of the response to different items
    D. tell the individual to try to make himself appear normal, then neurotic
    E. repeat certain questions in slightly different form throughout the test

15. Johnny, a twelve-year-old handicapped child, suddenly begins to suck his thumb and wet his bed soon after his newborn brother is brought home from the hospital. This psychological mechanism is known as

    A. introjection
    B. sublimation
    C. repression
    D. regression
    E. compensation

16. Six- and seven-year-old children are interested primarily in stories about

    A. family and school activities
    B. fairies and elves
    C. adventures on land and sea
    D. science and nature
    E. cowboys and Indians

17. The use of rewards is MOST productive in learning to the extent that they

    A. are concrete
    B. are used economically
    C. are delayed
    D. correspond to the work that has been done
    E. fulfill a need of the learner

18. In order to increase the chances that learned responses will be applied to new problem situations, the teacher should attempt, whenever possible, to

    A. provide clear objectives
    B. use concrete materials
    C. generalize patterns of response
    D. integrate subject matter areas
    E. use examples from everyday life

19. The pupil's readiness for any learning situation is the sum of all his characteristics which make him more likely to respond one way than another. Of these characteristics, the MOST important one generally is his

    A. interests
    B. physical health
    C. previous experience
    D. maturity
    E. perceptivity

20. It is generally assumed by clinical psychologists that the MOST serious behavior problems are manifested by children who

A. are most retarded
B. are most withdrawn
C. are most aggressive
D. cannot read
E. are overly dependent

21. Finger painting is enjoyed by many children. As a mechanism of adjustment, interest in finger painting may be looked upon as a form of 21.____

    A. projection
    B. conversion
    C. self-expression
    D. sublimation
    E. displacement

22. Personal problems in adjustment are MOST likely to arise in adolescent groups of 22.____

    A. early maturing girls and boys
    B. late maturing girls and boys
    C. early maturing girls and late maturing boys
    D. late maturing girls and early maturing boys
    E. all early and late maturing girls and boys

23. In establishing identity and sex role, the adolescent is MOST likely to be influenced by 23.____

    A. parents
    B. siblings
    C. peers
    D. ministers
    E. movie and baseball stars

24. Which one of the following judgments about parent-teenager relationships is FALSE? 24.____

    A. A parent's approval of work well done and overt pride in his child's accomplishment mean a great deal to the teenager, even though the latter may make light of it.
    B. To enhance ultimately the young person's self-respect, it is a good idea to criticize and question him as much as possible.
    C. Giving a teenager abundant opportunity to relate with a group has a positive effect on his school achievement.
    D. A parent's recognition and appreciation of good school progress, without exerting heavy pressure, serves to aid in maintaining this good record of accomplishment.
    E. A parent's realization that a major aspect of adolescent social development is the shift in interest and involvement from the family to the outside, with a concomitant desire and need for independence.

25. In learning theory terms, the psychoanalytic mechanism of displacement may be seen as an illustration of 25.____

    A. reinforcement
    B. discrimination
    C. extinction
    D. generalization
    E. assimilation

26. When an illness is described as psychosomatic, it means that the symptoms 26.____

    A. are psychological, but physiological factors contribute
    B. are physiological, but psychological factors contribute
    C. and all contributing factors are psychological
    D. and all contributing factors are physiological
    E. are both physiological and psychological

27. Most pronounced cases of bullying and aggressiveness are the result of efforts on the child's part to 27.____

A. impress adults with his strength
B. gain the attention of those around him
C. reach a level of achievement that is beyond him
D. compensate for deep feelings of inadequacy
E. create a "real-self" which corresponds to an "ideal-self"

28. Suzanne has received more votes than any other girl for student senate member. If she is typical of most of the girls who win this kind of recognition, she probably differs MOST from the average girl in the school in

    A. being emotionally more mature and balanced
    B. showing less competitive and aggressive tendencies
    C. making innovations without permission
    D. exhibiting more concern for herself and less awareness of the needs and problems of others
    E. being somewhat superior in aptitude and achievement

28.____

29. "I know what my parents expect of me; I know what teachers demand. I know what the other fellows in my crowd want me to do. I have a dim idea of what my girl wants from me. But I don't know what I want for myself." This statement illustrates the central adolescent problem of

    A. configuration
    B. peer group conformity
    C. acculturation
    D. introspection and inversion
    E. identity

29.____

30. The imaginative transposing of oneself into the thinking, feeling, and acting of another, and so structuring the world as he does, is an accurate definition of

    A. empathy   B. rapport
    C. conditioning   D. exclusion
    E. projection

30.____

31. A common change in the personality defenses of the adolescent child is the development of

    A. greater intellectualism and isolation of affect
    B. a tendency toward avoidance and denial
    C. suspicion and withdrawal
    D. repression and depression
    E. greater empathy and awareness of others

31.____

32. Tom has applied for several college scholarships, but has not obtained any. He says that none of the colleges really examine the candidates carefully or fairly. Which defense mechanism is he manifesting? That of

    A. rationalization   B. projection
    C. sublimation   D. repression
    E. introspection

32.____

33. When a person says, "I am so fond of you," when you know he actually dislikes you, there is reason to suspect that he is using the defense mechanism of

33.____

A. introjection
B. projection
C. rationalization
D. compensation
E. reaction formation

34. Of the following self-concepts, the MOST desirable one for a child to develop from the standpoint of mental health is

    A. whatever I do is good
    B. if I fail at something, it isn't important
    C. I know I have limitations; no one is perfect
    D. I must always be alert to my weaknesses
    E. I am capable of reaching my goals

35. Studies of children's fantasies show that, in the average elementary school child, fantasies

    A. play no significant part in his life
    B. will still be active but are becoming tempered with reality
    C. are an indication of an unsettled inner life
    D. are an indication that the child is unable to face his problems
    E. encourage the child to retreat from the demands of the world of reality

36. In collecting data for identifying pupil problems, information which compares a child to his peer group is called

    A. ideographic
    B. psychogenic
    C. psychodiagnostic
    D. normative
    E. sociometric

37. Of the following, what is the effect of a child's self-concept upon his behavior?

    A. It shifts and/or distorts the perceptions that act as stimuli to behavior.
    B. It functions principally in matters where conformity to or violation of the social code is involved.
    C. Its influence is best described by the Freudian concept of superego.
    D. It enables him to put his best foot forward.
    E. It helps the child to learn who he really is.

38. Compared to a group of unselected children of the same age, sex and race, gifted children, on the average,

    A. have a higher incidence of visual defects
    B. reach puberty later
    C. are taller, heavier and stronger
    D. show more personality problems
    E. are better "mixers"

39. Roger, who has a morbid fear of attending school and has been absent all year, is described as suffering from a(n)

    A. psychosis
    B. phobia
    C. inversion
    D. regression
    E. psychopathy

40. The term AMBIVALENT is used to describe a child who

   A. is given to creating dissension among others
   B. makes a statement and later amplifies it with conscious intent
   C. seems to be daydreaming while actually alert
   D. is aggressive at times and friendly at other times
   E. fearful in manner but overpowering in action

41. Transference is an important aspect of

   A. test construction
   B. grade placement
   C. anecdotal record keeping
   D. superior intelligence
   E. therapy

42. The term commonly used in statistics to refer to the average of a group of scores is the

   A. range
   B. mode
   C. central tendency
   D. median
   E. mean

43. A wound or injury to the emotions is called

   A. an illusion
   B. a trauma
   C. hysteria
   D. a delusion
   E. a syndrome

44. A child is psychotic who has a(n)

   A. urge toward some inappropriate sexual behavior
   B. nervous disorder of a functional type
   C. prolonged form of mental derangement
   D. inhibition in his social behavior
   E. physiogenic disorder

45. Individual differences in persons begin to be noticeable

   A. from birth onward
   B. after the child enters school
   C. when the child begins to communicate
   D. after visual-motor coordination has been achieved
   E. when the child begins to participate in competitive sports

46. In which one of the following statements is the mechanism of identification operating?

   A. "I'm not a good ballplayer, but I get good grades in arithmetic."
   B. "My teacher is always picking on me."
   C. "John was mad at me, but I'm bigger, so he pushed Sally, she's smaller."
   D. "I like blue dresses; my teacher wears blue a lot."
   E. "Of course I lost the tennis match; I was using a defective racket!"

47. In developing good character traits in young children, the BEST of the following techniques is probably

A. short dramatic discussions on good behavior
B. TV programs which have good behavior as "the moral"
C. administration of a personality test and follow-up discussion of the results
D. the desired type of behavior on the part of the adults with whom the children come into contact regularly
E. the emulation of outstanding personalities in the news, including athletes and actors

48. The term which MOST clearly expresses the psychological basis of modern educational practice is

   A. atomistic
   B. structuralistic
   C. analytic
   D. behavioristic
   E. organismic

49. Of the following possible first steps for helping an awkward child overcome his fear of playground activities, the one which is usually BEST is to

   A. give him some easy task connected with the game, "keeping score," for example
   B. send him to another classroom during the game period
   C. insist that he get into the game and play immediately
   D. allow him to work or do something else, alone
   E. encourage him to observe the game for a while with the hope that he will soon be motivated to play

50. Of the following, the MOST important consideration in distinguishing anxiety from fear is the

   A. intensity of the emotion
   B. extent of relation to subjective as distinguished from objective conditions
   C. strength of the personality organization of the one who is affected
   D. actuality of danger
   E. direction of the emotion

KEY (CORRECT ANSWERS)

1. C	11. E	21. D	31. A	41. E
2. C	12. D	22. C	32. A	42. E
3. D	13. A	23. C	33. E	43. B
4. C	14. A	24. B	34. E	44. C
5. A	15. D	25. D	35. B	45. A
6. C	16. A	26. B	36. D	46. D
7. D	17. E	27. D	37. A	47. D
8. B	18. C	28. C	38. C	48. E
9. A	19. D	29. E	39. B	49. A
10. B	20. B	30. A	40. D	50. B

TEST 2

DIRECTIONS: Each question or incomplete statement is followed by several suggested answers or completions. Select the one that BEST answers the question or completes the statement. *PRINT THE LETTER OF THE CORRECT ANSWER IN THE SPACE AT THE RIGHT.*

1. Research on sex differences in reading achievement indicates that 1.____

    A. more boys than girls suffer reading disabilities
    B. more girls than boys suffer reading disabilities
    C. there are no appreciable sex differences in reading achievement
    D. more boys than girls suffer reading disabilities in the elementary grades, but more girls than boys suffer reading disabilities in the secondary grades
    E. all such studies are statistically unreliable

2. Studies have shown that the ratio of reading disability among boys as compared to girls is 2.____

    A. 4 to 1   B. 3 to 1
    C. 2 to 1   D. equal
    E. slightly greater

3. The pecularities of language behavior in the schizophrenic arise from his extreme need of a feeling of 3.____

    A. personal security   B. self-denial
    C. disarticulation   D. isolation
    E. grandeur

4. Of the following, the LEAST effective way of dealing with children's fears is 4.____

    A. explaining and reassuring
    B. helping the child to face the feared situation
    C. simply ignoring the child's fear
    D. setting examples of fearlessness
    E. looking to the causes of the fear

5. The age at which individuals cease to grow in intellectual ability is 5.____

    A. 13 years   B. 16 years
    C. 21 years   D. 29 years
    E. probably none of these

6. Personality is the result of 6.____

    A. inheritance only
    B. environment only
    C. both inheritance and environment
    D. neither inheritance nor environment
    E. inheritance to a greater extent than environment

29

7. Children's groups about the age of two typically show 7.____

   A. much cooperation B. sex segregation
   C. parallel activity D. all of these
   E. none of these

8. Play and reading interests of boys and girls will be found to be MOST different at the age 8.____
   of

   A. three years B. six years
   C. ten years D. twelve years
   E. eighteen years

9. As children in groups with very limited environments, such as canal-boat dwellers, "hol- 9.____
   low-folk," etc., grow older, their I.Q. is found to

   A. increase
   B. increase greatly
   C. stay the same
   D. decrease
   E. vary widely and irregularly

10. A child reared in isolation will NOT naturally 10.____

    A. eat
    B. sleep
    C. talk
    D. take shelter
    E. investigate his surroundings

11. Although young children are egocentric, it has been found that social development 11.____

    A. is common among two-year-olds
    B. is well under way at the age of four
    C. is well under way at the age of five
    D. is not noticeable until the sixth-year level
    E. varies so greatly among children that it cannot be approximated at any one age

12. The rate and pattern of early motor development of children depend *mainly* upon 12.____

    A. experience B. acculturation
    C. maturation D. training
    E. personal aptitude

13. For optimum individual and social growth, children should be encouraged to 13.____

    A. initiate their own activities
    B. accept the choices and decisions of their peers
    C. learn to play alone
    D. respect the leaders in the class
    E. participate in clubs and groups led by children of their own age

14. Most young adolescents 14._____

    A. struggle to establish themselves as important members of the family but question family controls
    B. struggle to establish themselves as important members of the family and accept family controls without question
    C. are content with secondary roles in the family provided the family relinquishes all controls over them
    D. prefer to be told what to do by parents in order to be relieved of all responsibility for making decisions
    E. accept family controls when the rules are set by the father, but question and often disobey controls set by the mother

15. Because boys and girls of junior high school age become increasingly interested in the opposite sex, the teacher should 15._____

    A. seat them apart so that they can concentrate on their work
    B. encourage "dating"
    C. group the students with members of their own sex for all committee work
    D. forbid the use of all cosmetics in class
    E. teach the social amenities

16. On the whole, if junior high school children are treated as responsible young people, 16._____

    A. they will do what is expected of them
    B. they will react by giggling
    C. the teacher will lose control of the class
    D. their parents will object because they are not yet ready for responsibility
    E. they will assume that they are not amenable to ordinary school regulations

17. The adolescent is MOST likely to seek the greatest emotional support and understanding from 17._____

    A. idealized adults   B. isolated activity
    C. religious authorities   D. heterosexual interactions
    E. the peer culture

18. Emotional reactions are so important in behavior disorders because they are 18._____

    A. very intense
    B. not readily changed from infancy to adulthood
    C. varying in form from person to person
    D. so easily learned
    E. difficult to communicate and share socially

19. At the adolescent level, "adjustment" usually depends MOST strongly on having 19._____

    A. respect from parents
    B. adequate sex education
    C. average school achievement or better
    D. warm approval from teachers
    E. acceptance from peers

20. The fantasies of a child are MOST often used by a psychologist as a clue to his   20.____

    A. level of maturity   B. inner needs
    C. social adjustment   D. intelligence
    E. emotional stability

21.   I. The social and emotional adjustment of the child of six to eight depends in a   21.____
          major way on the security of the home.
       II. Children tend to form stereotypes and to focus on the unusual.
    The CORRECT answer is:

    A. Both I and II are correct
    B. Both I and II are incorrect
    C. I is correct; II is incorrect
    D. I is incorrect; II is correct
    E. One cannot draw a conclusion

22. The psychological climate of the home which influences adjustment of the child is MOST   22.____
    closely related to the

    A. number of children in the home
    B. educational level of the parents
    C. occupational level of the father
    D. attitudes of the parents
    E. socio-economic status of the family

23. Of the following characteristics, the one MOST generally found among children just   23.____
    entering the junior high schools is

    A. a tendency of boys and girls to seek each other's company
    B. the acceptance of parent and teacher opinion with little question
    C. the popularity of guessing games, puzzles, and games of choice
    D. a preference for highly organized competitive team play
    E. a conscientious and ardent effort to achieve academic success

24. Studies of child growth indicate that   24.____

    A. the onset of puberty adversely effects the child's motor coordination
    B. mentally retarded children are usually above norms in physical growth
    C. each child has his own growth pattern
    D. mental growth and physical growth are highly correlated
    E. physical growth and emotional stability are highly correlated

25. Which of the following statements is LEAST likely to be TRUE of first grade children as   25.____
    compared with fifth graders?

    A. There is much concern for group welfare and group approval.
    B. There is little concern for order and neatness.
    C. Some regular routines give security to children of this age.
    D. There is little intermingling of boys and girls in their play activities.
    E. There is a dislike for oral reading.

26. Most differences in play activities and interests between boys and girls in the elementary school years can probably be attributed to

    A. inherent biological differences
    B. inherent emotional differences
    C. instinctual influences
    D. cultural influences
    E. inherent intellectual differences

27. As part of the socialization process, the phenomenon of ambivalence is at its highest intensity during the

    A. toddler years
    B. preschool years
    C. early school years
    D. intermediate school years
    E. high school years

28. In early childhood, the individual tends to pattern himself on or to identify himself MOST generally with

    A. glamorous or romantic figures
    B. age contemporaries
    C. characters in movies or on TV
    D. parents or parent substitutes
    E. teachers

29. With respect to physical growth, superior children as compared with children of average intelligence are

    A. markedly inferior   B. slightly inferior
    C. slightly superior   D. about average
    E. markedly superior

30. Wishes of children of elementary school age deal mainly with

    A. improvement of their own inner strength, character or intelligence
    B. exploitation of family relationships
    C. possessions, pleasant experiences, privileges, opportunities for enjoyment
    D. improvement of their personal appearance
    E. improvement of their physical strength and prowess

31. With reference to emotional stability, intellectually gifted children as a group compared to average children are

    A. generally inferior   B. unpredictably related
    C. generally superior   D. predictably related
    E. the same

32. In comparing the rate of biological growth for boys and girls between the ages of 5-7 and 7-10, the latter period shows

    A. a slightly more accelerated rate than the former
    B. a slightly less accelerated rate than the former
    C. a rate equal to the former period

D. a markedly more accelerated rate than the former
E. a markedly less accelerated rate than the former

33. Of the following, the MOST important determinant of leadership in pre-adolescent children is the child's

   A. self-confidence
   B. sex
   C. physical attractiveness
   D. socio-economic status
   E. mental abilities

34. Marked improvement in a child's ability to draw a man over a period of time is MOST likely to be related to

   A. better social adjustment
   B. maturational effect
   C. the overcoming of a reading disability
   D. recovery from an illness
   E. better muscular coordination

35. As a means of changing the current behavior pattern of an adolescent, which of the following forces will generally prove to be MOST potent? Disapproval of the behavior pattern by

   A. the adolescent's parents
   B. an adult he admires
   C. a group of his peers
   D. his classroom teacher
   E. a close sibling

36. Of the following, the characteristic that is MOST important in determining an individual's status in a group of pre-adolescent girls is her

   A. school achievement
   B. socio-economic status
   C. ability to make friends
   D. intelligence
   E. physical appearance

37. The main advantage of the cross-sectional study over the longitudinal study in child development research is that the former

   A. permits an analysis of the growth of each child
   B. allows for an examination of individual and child growth increments
   C. allows for a detailed analysis of the interrelations among growth processes
   D. involves fewer sampling difficulties
   E. yields more accurate results by studying a larger sample

38. The greatest "social distance" in boy-girl relationships has been found to be during the ages

   A. 13 to 17 years
   B. 9 to 13 years
   C. 2 to 5 years
   D. 5 to 9 years
   E. 17 to 19 years

39. Of the following, the MOST frequent reason why two 11-year old boys stop "being friends" is

   A. lack of agreement concerning activities to be undertaken
   B. lack of recent contact
   C. parental disapproval
   D. a clash of personalities
   E. changing interests

40. A recent comprehensive survey of child-rearing patterns in America found mothers of the working class when compared in their toilet-training practices with mothers of the upper-middle class to be

   A. more permissive
   B. more accepting
   C. more severe
   D. more indifferent
   E. more uninformed

41. The leisure time activities of the typical pre-adolescent boys' group is mainly given over to

   A. a succession of activities suited to a changing number of players
   B. just "hanging around with the boys"
   C. games governed by a highly organized series of rules
   D. aimless circulation over a relatively large area looking for something to do
   E. a succession of activities suited to a limited number of players and games governed by few, if any, rules

42. Of the following, the MOST important symptom indicative of the social and emotional maladjustment of problem pupils is

   A. whispering and fooling while work is going on
   B. association with a gang
   C. destroying your neighbor's work
   D. inability to assume responsibility
   E. shyness and daydreaming

43. Of the following types of behavior, psychiatrists consider the MOST serious to be

   A. profanity
   B. smoking
   C. unsociability
   D. whispering in class
   E. dependence

44. The MOST impelling reason for young adolescents' use of slang is

   A. ignorance
   B. hearing it at home
   C. the desire to attain peer status through its use
   D. the attraction of its colorful expressions
   E. rebellion against the accepted media of speech

45. Sibling rivalry is the term used to describe the competitive feeling between two or more individuals who 45.____
    A. are in the same school grade
    B. are children of the same parents
    C. have similar goals of achievement
    D. are in the same chronological age group
    E. are identical twins

KEY (CORRECT ANSWERS)

1. A	11. B	21. A	31. C	41. A
2. B	12. B	22. D	32. B	42. B
3. A	13. B	23. C	33. A	43. C
4. C	14. A	24. C	34. A	44. C
5. E	15. E	25. A	35. C	45. B
6. C	16. A	26. D	36. C	
7. C	17. E	27. B	37. D	
8. D	18. E	28. D	38. B	
9. D	19. E	29. C	39. B	
10. C	20. B	30. C	40. C	

EXAMINATION SECTION
TEST 1

DIRECTIONS: Each question or incomplete statement is followed by several suggested answers or completions. Select the one that BEST answers the question or completes the statement. *PRINT THE LETTER OF THE CORRECT ANSWER IN THE SPACE AT THE RIGHT.*

1. The peer group serves the individual in the socialization process by

    A. showing him how to relate to other groups
    B. showing him how to be mature
    C. helping him to achieve an identity for himself
    D. helping him accept the discipline of his family

2. The age at which intelligence tests yield the MOST reliable prediction of future academic performance is

    A. 2-4   B. 4-6   C. 6-8   D. 12-14

3. Many studies have explored the effects of maternal deprivation on children. The findings indicate that such deprived children are MOST likely to be

    A. independent and active
    B. inert, withdrawn, mentally retarded and physically inferior
    C. less prone to infectious diseases because there is less danger of infection from others
    D. socially responsive to other adults

4. Of the following, which is MOST characteristic of the late maturing adolescent boy?

    A. Better adjustment to his age mates
    B. Greater independence of others
    C. Better acceptance of discipline
    D. Consistently negative evaluation of himself

5. Of the following, the major cause of juvenile delinquency is

    A. parental rejection   B. poverty
    C. culture conflict   D. inferior biological structure

6. In the recent research and study concerning the learning of disadvantaged youth, the MOST important single finding has been that

    A. the pre-school is the level of education which must be expanded
    B. the mother is the key factor in the enrichment of the socially disadvantaged
    C. the model the child identifies with must be well chosen
    D. little can be done for delinquent girls after seventeen years of age

7. An author who concerns himself with the "epigenetic principle of gradual unfoldings," the principle that the successive differentiations made during a lifetime provide a person with a developmental concept of self, is

    A. Esther Lloyd-Jones   B. Erik Erikson
    C. John Dewey   D. Edmund G. Williamson

8. The belief that power and status motives are MORE significant for behavior than broadly sexual motives was advocated by

   A. Freud
   B. Adler
   C. Jung
   D. Rank

9. Of all children, what percentage is generally considered to be mentally retarded?

   A. .5   B. 3.0   C. 10.0   D. 15.0

10. Studies of social acceptance show that gifted children are

    A. less socially acceptable than the average
    B. more socially acceptable than the retarded but less socially acceptable than the average
    C. more socially acceptable than the average and far more than the retarded
    D. no more socially accepted than the average

11. Of the following, the major characteristic of autistic type schizophrenic children is

    A. psychosomatic symptoms
    B. extreme withdrawal tendencies
    C. psychopathic symptoms
    D. extreme suspiciousness of adults

12. Of the following, the protective test MOST useful in studying the body-image of crippled children is the

    A. CHILDREN'S APPERCEPTION TEST
    B. BLACKY TEST
    C. MACHOVER DRAW-A-PERSON
    D. HOUSE-TREE-PERSON

13. The MOST serious problem for the cerebral palsied which contributes to learning difficulty in school, next to speech, is

    A. defective vision
    B. left-handedness
    C. hearing
    D. hand and eye coordination

14. Of the following symptoms, which is MOST characteristic of brain damaged children?

    A. Perseveration
    B. Echolalia
    C. Hallucinations
    D. Anorexia

15. Of the following, the organization that would be MOST helpful in working with a child suffering from athetosis would be the

    A. Association for the Help of Retarded Children
    B. United Cerebral Palsy Association
    C. Parents' Association for CRMD
    D. League for Epilepsy

16. The behavior patterns that develop during adolescence are

    A. genetically determined
    B. culturally determined
    C. physiologically determined
    D. found in all societies

17. According to Erikson, if a child has his needs thoroughly satisfied during his childhood, he is *most likely* to be an adolescent who is

    A. over-demanding
    B. unable to meet frustration
    C. over-achieving
    D. successful in personal-social development

18. Research evidence on girls' fears indicates that their fears during the oepidal period involve the type of anxiety known as

    A. separation
    B. fixation
    C. castration
    D. deprivation

19. In the University of Chicago study on identical twins reared apart, the GREATEST similarity found was in

    A. intelligence
    B. vocational choice
    C. personality
    D. physical appearance

20. In which of the following groups of adolescents are personal problems in adjustment MOST likely to arise?

    A. Early maturing boys and girls
    B. Late maturing boys and girls
    C. Early maturing girls and late maturing boys
    D. Late maturing girls and early maturing boys

21. The adolescent gang structure fulfills the unsatisfied needs of lower class youth through his acquisition of

    A. social skills
    B. intellectual and vocational interests
    C. athletic skills
    D. sanctions for his own aggression

22. The major limitation of the sociogram and sociometric test is that it does NOT disclose the

    A. status of the individual
    B. variety of choice
    C. organization pattern
    D. factors underlying choice

23. In establishing identity and sex role, the adolescent is MOST likely to be influenced by which of the following?

    A. Parents
    B. Siblings
    C. Peers
    D. Teachers

24. Studies on the characteristics of intellectually dull adolescents indicate

   A. inferior physical development on the part of the dull as compared with normal children
   B. more frequent eye, ear and speech defects among the dull children
   C. no clear social or emotional difference between dull and normal children
   D. all of the above characteristics to be true

25. "I made the varsity basketball and football teams but the coach cut me off the track squad." This statement embodies which of the following ego-defense mechanisms?

   A. Projection
   B. Sublimation
   C. Repression
   D. Regression

26. Considering the various informal groups which exist in a school system, such as faculty friendship groups, student clubs, cliques, and gangs, it is noticeable that the members of each group tend to possess common information and common ideas in many respects. These group beliefs exist because

   A. of the initial self-selection of the group by its members
   B. information is filtered through group leaders
   C. members are subjected to the same range of information
   D. all of the above are true

27. Of the following, the information that a sociogram does NOT reveal is the

   A. general pattern of group organization
   B. network of group communication
   C. reasons for choices and rejections
   D. relative strength of choice status of individual members

28. The weaknesses in cross-sectional studies of adolescents lie in the fact that

   A. only those who survive through the high school are sampled
   B. only the lower levels of the socio-economic groups are sampled
   C. only some interrelationships of the aspects of growth are studied
   D. the lower levels of ability are also sampled

29. The stimulus-response theory of learning explains behavior in terms of

   A. subliminal motivational cues
   B. heredity and environment
   C. physiological processes
   D. learning by insight

30. Of the following, the major weakness of a sociometric test of social acceptability that asks only for positive choices is that it

   A. has a bad mental hygiene effect on the class
   B. crystallizes the groups' opinions of each other
   C. will give a good picture of the children in the middle range of acceptability
   D. fails to distinguish between the "overlooked" children and those who are rejected

31. In "Jonesville," middle class adolescents asked to name their best friends usually chose someone   31._____

    A. of their own social class
    B. of higher status than their own
    C. below them in social status
    D. they liked for personal reasons; their choices were distributed among all social classes

32. A common change in the personality defenses of the adolescent child is the development of   32._____

    A. greater intellectualism and isolation of affect
    B. a tendency toward avoidance and denial
    C. suspicion and withdrawal
    D. repression and literal-mindedness

33. Studies on the development of sex characteristics during pubescent growth indicate that   33._____

    A. the sequence in the development of sex characteristics is marked by great consistency
    B. the age at which specific sex characteristics appear is quite reliable
    C. the only differences in the age occurrence of specific characteristics is due to sex differences
    D. there is little range in size or variability of sex characteristics

34. Adler, Horney, and Rank are deviationists from which one of the following theories?   34._____

    A. Psychoanalytical   B. Rogerian
    C. Communications   D. Neobehavioral

35. All of the following are identified with behavioral counseling EXCEPT   35._____

    A. Williamson   B. Skinner
    C. Eysenck   D. Krumboltz

36. All of the following associations are correct EXCEPT   36._____

    A. endomorphy - softness and spherical appearance
    B. mesomorphy - hard and rectangular physique with a predominance of bone and muscle
    C. ectomorphy - a linear and fragile physique
    D. gynandromorphy - a physique that represents an exaggeration of sexual characteristics associated with the given sex

37. Psychiatrists generally agree that the three characteristics *usually* combined in a severely troubled child are   37._____

    A. laziness, hostility, withdrawal
    B. slight height, overweight, pallor
    C. lack of relatedness, a speech problem, an eating problem
    D. undernourishment, fatigue, lack of coordination

38. Directing an emotion toward a safe or acceptable object as a substitute for a dangerous or unacceptable object is a fairly good definition for which one of the following defense mechanisms?

    A. Displacement
    B. Repression
    C. Identification
    D. Rationalization

39. The "latency period" as a concept of psychoanalysis has reference to the

    A. years between early childhood and adolescence
    B. period during which successful toilet training (accommodation to time, place and manner) is normally achieved
    C. period during which the oedipal strivings reach their peak
    D. period of pubertal development

40. An unpopular girl frequently calls attention to the social deficiencies in others. Her behavior illustrates

    A. regression
    B. projection
    C. repression
    D. rationalization

41. Which one of the following was NOT supported by Kurt Lewin's research?

    A. People are more apt to change if they participate in a decision to change.
    B. It is easier to change individuals in a group situation rather than singly.
    C. Change brought about through groups was more lasting than that brought about singly.
    D. While pressures of group members upon individuals were very strong, they were not as influential as those of group leaders.

42. A six-year-old child should normally be expected to do all of the following EXCEPT

    A. play simple games
    B. put on a sweater without help
    C. draw with a crayon
    D. write in sentences

43. An educational television program developed especially for pre-school age children is

    A. Learning Your A B C's
    B. Sesame Street
    C. The Number Game
    D. The Partridge Family

44. Which of the following statements concerning masturbation in children is NOT true?

    A. Excessive masturbation can injure a child's genitals.
    B. Masturbation is practiced by most children at some point of their development.
    C. Masturbation may be a symptom of tenseness and nervousness in a child.
    D. There tends to be an increased urge to masturbate during adolescence.

45. A child's rate of physical growth is MOST rapid during the period

    A. from birth to two years
    B. from six to nine years
    C. of pre-adolescence
    D. of adolescence

46. In planning activities for a group of ten-year-old children, the children's counselor should   46.____

    A. encourage the children to participate in the planning
    B. schedule activities that are the easiest to plan
    C. realize that children at this age like to watch television
    D. insist that each child participate in each activity

47. A child of twelve would be MOST likely to find an outlet for his aggressive tendencies in   47.____

    A. watching television
    B. participating in athletics
    C. reading a history book
    D. playing checkers

48. Of the following, the statement which MOST accurately describes the physical development of boys and girls during adolescence is that   48.____

    A. girls generally mature earlier than boys
    B. boys generally mature earlier than girls
    C. boys and girls generally mature at about the same age
    D. physically active boys and girls generally mature earlier than physically inactive ones

49. The average child has not developed all the many abilities needed for beginning reading until the age of about   49.____

    A. two   B. four   C. six   D. eight

50. Which of the following situations indicates that the child is probably emotionally disturbed?   50.____

    A. A five-year-old girl suddenly starts behaving like a baby after the birth of her sister.
    B. A four-year-old boy keeps asking for his father, although he has been told repeatedly that his father has died.
    C. A ten-year-old boy has refused to play with other children since he first entered school five years ago.
    D. All of the above

KEY (CORRECT ANSWERS)

1. C	11. B	21. D	31. B	41. D
2. C	12. C	22. D	32. A	42. D
3. B	13. D	23. C	33. A	43. B
4. D	14. A	24. D	34. A	44. A
5. A	15. B	25. A	35. A	45. A
6. A	16. B	26. D	36. D	46. A
7. B	17. D	27. C	37. C	47. B
8. B	18. C	28. A	38. A	48. A
9. B	19. D	29. C	39. A	49. C
10. C	20. C	30. D	40. B	50. C

TEST 2

DIRECTIONS: Each question or incomplete statement is followed by several suggested answers or completions. Select the one that BEST answers the question or completes the statement. *PRINT THE LETTER OF THE CORRECT ANSWER IN THE SPACE AT THE RIGHT.*

1. The process by which children take to themselves the values, the thinking, and social behavior of their parents is called

    A. projection
    B. identification
    C. fixation
    D. sublimation

    1._____

2. Of the following, the characteristic that MOST clearly differentiates primary drives from secondary drives is that primary drives

    A. are related to biological needs that must be satisfied
    B. are learned early in the developmental cycle
    C. are derived from complex patterns of behavior
    D. may be observed after biological needs have been met

    2._____

3. Spitz and Goldfarb, in two different studies, have suggested that children who will have predictably lower I.Q's are those reared in

    A. institutions
    B. broken homes
    C. foster homes
    D. middle class homes

    3._____

4. One of the MOST common fears of early childhood is the fear of

    A. animals
    B. being separated from parents
    C. being rejected by peers
    D. having too much independence

    4._____

5. The average child shows the FIRST signs of laughing responses

    A. before the age of six months
    B. between the ages of six months and one year
    C. at the age of about one year
    D. at the age of about fifteen months

    5._____

6. A child is LEAST likely to choose a child of the opposite sex to play with at the age of

    A. two
    B. four
    C. seven
    D. ten

    6._____

7. When toilet training a two-year-old child, the children's counselor should

    A. scold the child when she wets her pants
    B. take the child to the bathroom only when she asks to go
    C. have the child sit on the toilet for long periods of time
    D. keep the toilet training routine free from tension

    7._____

8. The average child of three years MOST often shows his anger by

    A. breaking things
    B. crying
    C. threatening his mother
    D. sulking

9. Children at the age of two or three occasionally have temper tantrums when they do not get what they want. Of the following, the BEST method for a children's counselor to use when faced with a temper tantrum by a two-year-old child in her group is to

    A. allow the child to have what he wants
    B. try to reason with the child by explaining why he cannot have what he wants
    C. wait until the worst of the temper tantrum is over and then make a friendly gesture toward the child
    D. order the child to stop this behavior

10. All of the following are good principles to follow in administering punishment to a three-year-old child EXCEPT the

    A. punishment should be administered immediately after the incident of bad behavior
    B. child should be punished only if he understands why his behavior was bad
    C. specific punishment should be appropriate to the specific case of bad behavior
    D. punishment should be administered in an impartial manner

11. Helen, a 14-year-old girl, has two younger sisters who are more successful than she in school. Her mother complains that at home Helen constantly makes remarks intended to hurt their feelings. Helen's behavior is BEST characterized as a form of

    A. compulsion
    B. sublimation
    C. rationalization
    D. projection

12. Overlearning is primarily an outgrowth of

    A. removal of inhibitions
    B. additional practice
    C. strong motivation
    D. fear of failure

13. "The mind responds to relationships, not to fixed stimuli" is associated with the movement in psychology known as

    A. associationism
    B. behaviorism
    C. Gestalt psychology
    D. functionalism

14. Which one of the following is an example of "projection"?

    A. Calling other people hostile although the hostility is within oneself
    B. Playing sick in order to avoid responsibility
    C. Kicking the desk when one really wants to kick the teacher
    D. Giving other than the true reason for one's behavior

15. The basketball player who was dropped from the squad says, "Now I'll have time to study." If he really wanted to make the team, he is

    A. regressing
    B. repressing
    C. projecting
    D. rationalizing

16. Which one of the following reactions is generally instigated by frustration?

    A. Tolerance B. Aggression
    C. Identification D. Avoidance

17. A patient asserts, "I can't stand the agony I suffer when I go against my mother's wishes." The therapist replies, "You really like to punish that momma inside of you for your dependency, don't you?" This response can be viewed as an example of

    A. reassurance B. interpretation
    C. support D. reflection of feeling

18. A shy young first-grade boy becomes extremely attached to his teacher. He brings her presents, asks her to help him with his clothing a great deal, and wants to sit near her all the time. He is MOST likely manifesting the mental mechanism of

    A. introjection B. sublimation
    C. reaction-formation D. transference

19. When Billy was told he could not have a cookie, he lay down on the floor and pounded it with his fists. This could be an example of

    A. repression B. inhibition
    C. overcompensation D. regression

20. Habit formations in children such biting nails, picking at sores, masturbating, etc. are generally the result of

    A. poor parental supervision and training
    B. local irritations
    C. impaired general health
    D. emotional tensions

21. The attention span of a young child

    A. is not related to his mental ability
    B. can be increased if he has a high I.Q.
    C. cannot be changed before the child learns to read
    D. can be increased if the child is interested in what he is doing

22. Most young children need

    A. few media of expression
    B. to engage in independent planning
    C. many concrete experiences
    D. generalized explanations

23. The person with whom it is MOST important for a five-year-old child to have a good adjustment is

    A. father B. mother
    C. teacher D. sibling

24. At five, the normal, average child is able to play BEST

    A. alone
    B. in a large group
    C. with one other child somewhat older than himself
    D. in a small group of five or six children

25. Good education for five-year-old children stresses the importance of 25.____

    A. learning to sit still and wait for a turn
    B. opportunities to develop skill in crafts
    C. opportunities to explore and experiment
    D. learning to walk with a partner in line

26. Motor activities figure MOST importantly in a young child's intellectual enterprises because, through them, he 26.____

    A. learns how to meet new situations successfully
    B. acquires concepts of size, shape, balance, proportion
    C. learns how to live happily with other children
    D. gains confidence in himself as a person

27. Children can BEST be helped to make good choices through 27.____

    A. play with peers
    B. many experiences in making choices
    C. absorbing the teacher's sense of values
    D. imitating other children older than they

28. The timid, shy child who hesitates to join in activities and use of materials 28.____

    A. should be left alone
    B. should be praised for the work he does by himself
    C. should be drawn into the group and encouraged to participate as often as possible
    D. should have his mother come to his class to visit so that he will have a feeling of security

29. To understand the emotional life of the adolescent, it is MOST important to 29.____

    A. appraise the adolescent's emotions in the light of our own experience
    B. take into account the many forces, apparent as well as hidden, that operate in his life
    C. overlook impulsive behavior without apparent motive
    D. draw up a scholastic profile

30. The youngster who says, "I got an A in mathematics, but the teacher gave me a D in reading," is manifesting behavior which may be termed 30.____

    A. identification   B. projection
    C. regression   D. repression

31. Of the following comments which might be made by a teacher to a boy who has just misbehaved, the one likely to be MOST effective in correcting the behavior is: 31.____

    A. You are a bad boy who likes to misbehave.
    B. You are a silly boy and don't know how to behave.
    C. You are a poor, foolish boy who will get in trouble.
    D. You are a good boy but you made a mistake.

32. The personality development of young children is hampered MOST by

    A. the lack of good schools manned by adequately educated teachers
    B. dissension in the family
    C. the lack of love and affection
    D. failure in school I

33. It has been found that the gap between ability and achievement is generally SMALLEST in the

    A. gifted pupil
    B. dull pupil
    C. average pupil
    D. pupil of high socio-economic background

34. Extreme deviations in motor, adaptive, or language expression or personal-social behavior are

    A. a definite indication that a child is subnormal
    B. cause for alarm on the part of parent and teacher
    C. an indication of a temporary maladjustment
    D. reasons for seeking the advice of a specialist

35. Children's groups about the age of two typically show

    A. much cooperation
    B. sex segregation
    C. parallel activity
    D. all of these

36. Play and reading interests of boys and girls will be found to be MOST different at the age of

    A. three years
    B. six years
    C. ten years
    D. twelve years

37. As children in groups with very limited environments, such as canal-boat dwellers, "hollow-folk," etc., grow older, their I.Q. is found to

    A. increase
    B. increase greatly
    C. stay the same
    D. decrease

38. Transfer from one subject to another or to life situations will be increased if

    A. techniques and applications are emphasized
    B. the first subject is very difficult
    C. a good deal of drill is given in the first subject
    D. the situations seem quite different

39. A contemporary book by Sheldon and Eleanor Glueck reports their findings of a careful research study of juvenile delinquents. They state that

    A. most of their delinquents showed anti-social behavior beginning with their sixth year
    B. most of their delinquents did not show anti-social behavior until after their eleventh year
    C. the delinquents showed more physical defects than non-delinquents
    D. prediction tables can help to detect potential delinquents

40. Finger sucking in early childhood has long been a subject of discussion among psychiatrists. The one of the following statements which is GENERALLY accepted as true is that
    A. finger sucking denotes pending neuroses and the parents need psychiatric consultation
    B. finger sucking is a normal activity of early childhood and should not be interfered with
    C. finger sucking alters the child's facial contours and should be heavily discouraged
    D. finger sucking by a child over nine months old is due to emotional upset and needs treatment

KEY (CORRECT ANSWERS)

1. B	11. D	21. D	31. D
2. A	12. B	22. C	32. C
3. A	13. C	23. B	33. B
4. B	14. A	24. D	34. D
5. A	15. D	25. C	35. C
6. D	16. B	26. B	36. D
7. D	17. B	27. B	37. D
8. B	18. D	28. C	38. A
9. C	19. D	29. B	39. D
10. B	20. D	30. B	40. B

EXAMINATION SECTION
TEST 1

DIRECTIONS: Each question or incomplete statement is followed by several suggested answers or completions. Select the one that BEST answers the question or completes the statement. *PRINT THE LETTER OF THE CORRECT ANSWER IN THE SPACE AT THE RIGHT.*

1. The psychologist whose name is MOST often associated with the theory that the experience of birth has a profound influence on personality development and that an individual who has a slow, prolonged birth is likely to have a personality which fights, struggles and plunges is

    A. Horney
    B. Freud
    C. Sullivan
    D. Rank

2. Which of the following is the MOST correct statement concerning puberty and physical maturity?

    A. Boys and girls who experience early puberty will achieve physical maturity and cease growing later than will the late maturers.
    B. Boys and girls who experience early puberty will achieve physical maturity and cease growing sooner than will the late maturers.
    C. Boys and girls who experience early puberty will achieve physical maturity and cease growing at approximately the same time as the late maturers.
    D. None of the above

3. The MOST prominent difficulties of the middle years of childhood revolve around

    A. relations with peer groups
    B. parent-child relationships
    C. schooling and the ability to learn
    D. physical development

4. In the normal population, the range of achievement of children of the same age in grades 5 and 6 is approximately from

    A. 1 to 2 years
    B. 2 to 4 years
    C. 3 to 5 years
    D. 5 to 8 years

5. The MOST accurate statement concerning anxiety, of the following, is that anxiety is

    A. needed for the socialization process
    B. not needed for the socialization process
    C. less produced by "mental" punishment than by physical punishment
    D. of negligible effect in producing neurosis

6. Of the following, the area of greatest similarity among children is in their

    A. inherited traits
    B. rates of development
    C. sequences of development
    D. patterns of growth dimensions

7. Of the following, which is the MOST significant factor in determining the choice of friends among children between the ages of six and ten?

    A. Mutual interests
    B. Similar personality traits
    C. Conveniently close location
    D. Social and economic standing of parents

8. Lewin, in defining his structural concepts of psychology, represented them

    A. topologically
    B. metrically
    C. geometrically
    D. orthographically

9. As part of the socialization process, the phenomenon of ambivalence is at its highest intensity during the

    A. toddler years
    B. preschool years
    C. early school years
    D. intermediate school years

10. The child's need to be a "goody-goody" and his willingness to conform are MOST frequently observed during the

    A. phallic period
    B. latency period
    C. prepubertal period
    D. adolescent period

11. Joe Flirp is a great health education teacher, to a large extent, because the boys model themselves after him. The foregoing illustrates the psychological mechanism of

    A. sublimation
    B. displacement
    C. regression
    D. identification

12. "You're much too authoritarian," said the principal to the teacher. "And I won't stand for that in my school." The principal is demonstrating the psychological mechanism of

    A. sublimation
    B. conversion
    C. projection
    D. identification

13. Margaret Snorble, unhappy because of her lack of friendship, devoted all her energy to studying. She became the number one student in her grade. Margaret is demonstrating the psychological mechanism of

    A. sublimation
    B. conversion
    C. introjection
    D. fantasy

14. Ben was ill now and then. However, each time after a short rest, he quickly became well. This tendency or process is known as

    A. redintegration
    B. regression
    C. homeostasis
    D. somatistation

15. Joanie asked for apple pie and was told that there was none left. "Oh, well," said she, "give me peach pie. I like it better anyway." Joanie is demonstrating the psychological mechanism of

    A. regression
    B. displacement
    C. rationalization
    D. sublimation

16. The principal had just left after telling Miss Jones she had to improve the quality of her lesson plans. Tears came to her eyes; she stamped her foot several times, pounded on the desk and then broke into uncontrolled sobbing. Miss Jones' behavior is an example of the psychological mechanism of

    A. introjection
    B. projection
    C. sublimation
    D. regression

16.____

17. Of the following statements concerning praise and punishment, which is LEAST in accord with modern psychological principles?

    A. When a child is bad, spank him.
    B. When a child is bad, say, "If you're not good, I won't love you any more."
    C. When a child is good, give him something to show your approval.
    D. When a child is good, say, "That's O.K. Let's try to do better next time."

17.____

18. Which one of the following is NOT characteristic of the development of a group?

    A. Emergence of collective goals
    B. Solidification of individual roles within the group structure
    C. Growth of group norms for behavior
    D. Development of a group atmosphere or social climate

18.____

19. The status of an individual in a group is determined, for the MOST part, by

    A. the possession of those qualities the group deems important
    B. his socio-economic level
    C. his status in other groups of which he is a member
    D. the amount of time and energy he is willing to devote to the purposes of the group

19.____

20. In comparison with other members of a group, the leader tends to

    A. hold himself in higher esteem
    B. be less spontaneous
    C. be more desirous of being of service to others
    D. be more willing to accept a low level of performance from members of the group

20.____

21. The individual who emerges as the leader of a group is usually

    A. the person who, in the judgment of the group, can best meet the demands of the particular problem
    B. superior to the other members of the group in a wide variety of abilities
    C. chosen on the basis of personal qualities rather than ability
    D. the same person, no matter in what activities the group participates

21.____

22. The degree of cohesiveness which has been established in a group is MOST likely to be lowered by

    A. unfavorable evaluation of the group by outsiders
    B. favorable evaluation of the group by outsiders
    C. decreasing the amount of interaction in the group
    D. increasing the degree of interaction in the group

22.____

23. Research has shown that neighborhood gangs tend to be more cohesive than groups of the same age functioning as clubs in more formal youth agencies. This would suggest that

    A. the club is potentially longer-lived than the gang
    B. young people join clubs only if they are not accepted by the gang
    C. clubs will not be able to function adequately in a given neighborhood until some way is found to destroy gangs already in existence
    D. the activities of the gang meet the needs of its members better than those of the club program do

24. Studies of the cohesiveness of small groups have indicated that the more cohesive a group, the

    A. more willing will the group be to defend itself against external criticism
    B. less likely is it that the group will permit internal disagreement with its objective or goals
    C. less perceptive is the group of its own solidarity
    D. more susceptible is the group to disruption caused by loss of a leader

25. According to Sullivan, anxiety serves as a defense against the danger of

    A. conditioned fears
    B. self-discovery
    C. destructive people on the outside
    D. interpersonal destructiveness

26. The system of classifying people into those who move towards, against, and away from people was devised by

    A. Alexander
    B. Fromm
    C. Fenichel
    D. Horney

27. Scientific investigators generally agree that the development of human behavior begins

    A. at the time of conception
    B. during the prenatal period
    C. at birth
    D. at the time of initial social interaction

28. Of the following, the MOST frequent reason why two 11-year old boys stop "being friends" is

    A. lack of agreement concerning activities to be undertaken
    B. lack of recent contact
    C. a clash of personalities
    D. parental disapproval

29. Of the following, the MOST important determinant of leadership in pre-adolescent children is the child's

    A. self-confidence
    B. sex
    C. physical attractiveness
    D. socio-economic status

30. Of the following, the one MOST likely to be associated with poor emotional development in a sixth-grade girl is   30._____

   A. lack of interest in boys
   B. striving for perfection in all her school work
   C. desire to please her parents in everything she does
   D. a strong interest in arithmetic, with only passive interest in other school subjects

31. The author of FOUNDATIONS OF READING INSTRUCTION is   31._____

   A. Paul Witty   B. Emmett A. Betts
   C. David H. Russell   D. Helen M. Robinson

32. The Dolch 220-word basic vocabulary consists of words that   32._____

   A. are most commonly used in fifteen basic readers on first and second grade levels
   B. are most commonly used in compositions by primary-grade children
   C. must be recognized as "sight words" because they do not follow regular phonetic principles
   D. make up fifty percent of reading matter used in the elementary schools

33. The MOST rapid rate of growth among children between the ages of 2 and 8 is found at age   33._____

   A. 2   B. 4   C. 6   D. 8

34. Studies of the relationship between sex and reading disability of elementary school pupils generally reveal that among pupils with reading disabilities the number of   34._____

   A. girls exceeds the number of boys
   B. boys and girls is about equal
   C. boys is slightly greater than the number of girls
   D. boys is about 3 times the number of girls

35. Research reports agree that the reading interests of groups of children   35._____

   A. begin to be different for boys and girls during the primary grades
   B. change consistently as children grow older
   C. center on animal stories during pre-adolescent years
   D. show no difference between boys and girls until junion high school years

36. The MOST accurate statement to make regarding the cause of reading disability is that research shows that most reading difficulties are primarily due to   36._____

   A. low intelligence
   B. familial discord
   C. insufficient motivation to read
   D. a complex of interrelated factors

37. Fernald's name is associated with a teaching procedure by which a child learns words by means of a   37._____

   A. look-and-say technique   B. visual motor approach
   C. tracing-and-writing procedure D. letter sound blending approach

38. A diagnostic report of a child's reading states that he has no word analysis techniques. 38.____
    This diagnosis is equivalent to saying that he

    A. has a poor meaningful vocabulary
    B. cannot understand what he reads
    C. cannot sound out words
    D. cannot adjust his rate

39. Where mixed dominance is identified as a possible causal factor for a child who makes 39.____
    many reversal errors, it would be BEST for the teacher to

    A. stress left to right direction in reading
    B. change the child's hand preference
    C. change the child's eye preference
    D. stress an oral approach in reading

40. The mother of a first-grade child is concerned about her child's reading. It appears that 40.____
    the child can read only the words in her primer, but cannot sound out any words not in
    her book. Of the following, the BEST explanation to the mother would be that

    A. it is all right because the children are not taught phonics today
    B. it is all right because the child will learn to sound words
    C. it is serious and the child will get special help soon
    D. it is all right since children are taught to read whole words first, then the sounds

41. As a means of changing the current behavior pattern of an adolescent, which of the fol- 41.____
    lowing forces will generally prove to be MOST potent? Disapproval of the behavior pat-
    tern by

    A. the adolescent's parents
    B. his classroom teacher
    C. a group of his peers
    D. an adult he admires

42. Of the following, the characteristic that is MOST important in determining an individual's 42.____
    status in a group of pre-adolescent girls is her

    A. school achievement   B. socio-economic status
    C. ability to make friends   D. intelligence

43. If the results of studies of boys' clubs are applicable to the school situation, one may 43.____
    expect the greatest amount of aggressive behavior to be noted in classes where the
    classroom climate may be described as

    A. permissive   B. laissez-faire
    C. democratic   D. autocratic

44. Which of the following authors would you be LEAST likely to recommend for information 44.____
    about child care?

    A. Sidonie Gruenberg   B. Jean Piaget
    C. Ernest Harms   D. Benjamin Spock

45. Of the following, which one is NOT an authority in reading? 45.____

    A. Gates B. Russell
    C. Harris D. Bullis

46. Studies have shown that the ratio of reading disability among boys as compared to girls is: 46.____

    A. 4 to 1 B. 3 to 1 C. 2 to 1 D. equal

47. Which of the following terms refers to the maintenance of stability in the physiological functioning of the organism? 47.____

    A. functional autonomy B. canalization
    C. homeostasis D. maturation

48. A recent comprehensive survey of child-rearing patterns in America found mothers of the working class when compared in their toilet-training practices with mothers of the middle class to be 48.____

    A. more permissive B. more indifferent
    C. more severe D. more accepting

49. Studies of the relationship of body build and character traits have in general been found to be 49.____

    A. positively correlated
    B. negatively correlated
    C. statistically significantly correlated
    D. inconclusive

50. The theory that psychical compensation for a feeling of physical or social inferiority is responsible for the development of a psychoneurosis is attributed to 50.____

    A. Adler B. Horney
    C. Freud D. Sullivan

KEY (CORRECT ANSWERS)

1. D	11. D	21. A	31. B	41. C
2. B	12. C	22. C	32. D	42. C
3. C	13. A	23. D	33. A	43. D
4. D	14. C	24. A	34. D	44. B
5. A	15. C	25. B	35. B	45. D
6. C	16. D	26. D	36. D	46. B
7. C	17. B	27. B	37. C	47. C
8. A	18. B	28. B	38. C	48. C
9. B	19. A	29. A	39. A	49. D
10. B	20. A	30. B	40. D	50. A

TEST 2

DIRECTIONS: Each question or incomplete statement is followed by several suggested answers or completions. Select the one that BEST answers the question or completes the statement. *PRINT THE LETTER OF THE CORRECT ANSWER IN THE SPACE AT THE RIGHT.*

1. Of the following, the MOST important consideration in distinguishing anxiety from fear is the

    A. intensity of the emotion
    B. extent of relation to subjective as distinguished from objective conditions
    C. actuality of danger
    D. strength of the personality organization of the one who is affected

2. Wishes of children of elementary school age deal mainly with

    A. improvement of their own inner strength, character, or intelligence
    B. improvement of their personal appearance
    C. possessions, pleasant experiences, privileges, opportunities for enjoyment
    D. exploitation of family relationships

3. The psychological climate of the home which influences adjustment of the child is MOST closely related to the

    A. number of children in the home
    B. educational level of the parents
    C. occupational level of the father
    D. attitudes of the parents

4. With reference to emotional stability, intellectually gifted children as a group compared to average children are

    A. generally inferior   B. the same
    C. generally superior   D. unpredictably related

5. Piaget distinguishes between two kinds of thought, logical and autistic. It is his thesis that the child's way of thinking is

    A. basically autistic
    B. either logical or autistic
    C. basically logical
    D. situated between the logical and the autistic

6. According to research findings, the MOST effective way to help a child deal with a specific fear, such as a fear of dogs, is to

    A. have the parents and others who are close to the child set an example of fearlessness
    B. explain matters to him in terms he can understand readily
    C. help him by degrees to come actively and directly to grips with the situation
    D. try to effect "positive reconditioning" by presenting the feared stimulus with an attractive one

7. A fundamental principle of the psychoanalytic school which has been accepted by most schools of psychology is the

   A. development of the collective unconscious
   B. theory of the existence of a dynamic unconscious
   C. development of an oedipus complex situation
   D. relationship between early psychosexual development and later adult behavior

8. In comparing the rate of biological growth for boys and girls between the ages of 5-7 and 7-10, the latter period shows

   A. a slightly more accelerated rate than the former
   B. a slightly less accelerated rate than the former
   C. a markedly more accelerated rate than the former
   D. a rate equal to the former period

9. The concept of "stages" in describing human development is LEAST applicable to

   A. Freud's psychoanalytic theory
   B. Piaget's cognitive theory
   C. Skinner's behavior theory
   D. Erikson's personality theory

10. The principal effect of nursery school attendance is upon the child's

    A. social development
    B. intellectual development
    C. perceptual development
    D. motor development

11. Which of the following terms is MOST clearly associated with stubborn reading disability?

    A. Apraxia   B. Dysplasia   C. Dyslexia   D. Aphasia

12. The boy who is encouraged or required to be more independent at an earlier age tends to develop a(n)

    A. low threshold for frustration
    B. inability to work well with others
    C. reluctance to accept adult authority
    D. strong need to achieve

13. Pioneering studies in eliminating children's fears were conducted by Mary Cover Jones. The methods used, which are consistent with present-day learning theory, included all but ONE of the following:

    A. Direct conditioning
    B. Social imitation
    C. Feeding responses
    D. Systematic desensitization

14. In contrast to upward mobile adolescents, downward mobile adolescents are

    A. less ambivalent in self-concept
    B. less interested in job security
    C. more confident in social relationships
    D. more dependent on their parents

15. In which of the following situations would a classroom atmosphere of competitiveness be   15.___
    LEAST detrimental to the cultivation of interpersonal relationships? Classmates are

    A. unfamiliar with one another, but equal in abilities
    B. familiar with one another and equal in abilities
    C. unfamiliar with one another and greatly disparate in abilities
    D. familiar with one another and greatly disparate in abilities

16. On group intelligence tests, Cyril Burt found the highest correlations between   16.___

    A. identical twins reared apart
    B. siblings reared together
    C. parents and own children living together
    D. identical twins reared together

17. An adolescent boy would like to have a girlfriend. As an example of sublimation, he might   17.___

    A. proclaim himself a "woman-hater"
    B. withdraw from all interpersonal relationships
    C. convince himself that girls are really crazy about him
    D. begin to write romantic poetry

18. Jim studies all night before an examination in an attempt to learn the entire course. This   18.___
    is an example of

    A. distributed practice   B. massed practice
    C. practice effect   D. spread of effect

19. The best-controlled studies of the influence of genetic factors on human behavior are   19.___
    found in investigations of

    A. newborn babies   B. identical twins
    C. fraternal twins   D. siblings

20. Terman's follow-up studies on a group of gifted children as compared to children of aver-   20.___
    age intelligence revealed them to have

    A. better adjustment as shown on personality and character tests
    B. greater physical problems
    C. lower incomes
    D. more uneven academic achievement

21. Which one of the following is the MOST important determinant of leadership among pre-   21.___
    adolescent boys?

    A. Intellectual ability
    B. Physical size and strength
    C. Popularity with girls
    D. Sensitivity to the needs of others

22. Billy wants to be admired, but he is too clumsy to achieve this goal through sports. Therefore, although not a bright pupil, he studies long hours and earns very high grades. This may be cited as an example of

    A. compensation
    B. projection
    C. rationalization
    D. reaction formation

23. Of the following, the MOST important factor making for the development of friendship among young children is

    A. similarity in interests
    B. similarity in social class
    C. geographic proximity
    D. friendship among parents

24. Harlow's work on mothering in monkeys suggests that the affective bond between the infant and the mother is based on

    A. feeding
    B. grooming
    C. tactile contact
    D. primitive vocalization

25. The CORRECT order of Piaget's developmental stages is

    A. concrete operations, preoperational, sensorimotor, formal operational
    B. concrete operations, sensorimotor, preoperational, formal operational
    C. sensorimotor, concrete operations, preoperational, formal operational
    D. sensorimotor, preoperational, concrete operations, formal operational

26. Piaget's process which states that children invent increasingly more and better schemata for adapting to their environment is known as

    A. assimilation
    B. equilibrium
    C. accommodation
    D. conservation

27. Which of the following is NOT considered by Erikson to be a developmental task of adolescence?

    A. Development of a sense of shared identity with another
    B. Development of sexual identity
    C. Ability to see one's life in perspective
    D. Experimentation with different roles

28. A six-year-old child who is able to solve a conservation problem would be classified under which of the following stages described by Piaget?

    A. Sensorimotor
    B. Formal operations
    C. Preoperational
    D. Concrete operations

29. During adolescence, girls *generally* surpass boys in

    A. scientific ability
    B. mathematical ability
    C. ability to perform verbal tasks
    D. gross motor skills

30. The CORRECT order of Freud's stages of psychosexual development is:

    A. Oral, latency, anal, phallic, genital
    B. Oral, anal, phallic, latency, genital
    C. Phallic, oral, anal, latency, genital
    D. Latency, oral, genital, anal, phallic

31. According to Erikson, a MAJOR developmental conflict a child faces in the elementary school age period is the conflict between

    A. initiative and guilt
    B. identity and identity diffusion
    C. industry and inferiority
    D. trust and mistrust

32. According to Piaget, in the preoperational stage children

    A. begin to classify and order activities internally
    B. begin to integrate sensory and motor activities
    C. gain the ability to think logically about a problem
    D. are unable to transcend the here and now and are dependent on immediate perception

33. A pupil is able to reason simultaneously about whole and part and is able to classify according to two or three properties. According to Piaget, the pupil is in the _____ stage.

    A. sensory-motor   B. formal operations
    C. preoperational   D. concrete operations

34. According to Kohlberg, moral development proceeds through a sequence of stages that are

    A. dependent on the individual's personality and the way in which society reacts to that personality
    B. strongly influenced by individual differences in educational experience and religious training
    C. characterized by increasing symmetry, conventionality, and objectivity
    D. universal and invariant from one culture to another

35. The technique in which a particular form or sequence of behavior is established by reinforcing successively closer approximations to that behavior is called

    A. discriminative responding
    B. shaping
    C. classical conditioning
    D. fading

36. The HIGHEST need in Maslow's hierarchy of human needs is

    A. safety   B. love
    C. self-actualization   D. integration

37. According to Piaget, a child's thinking becomes completely general and capable of dealing with the hypothetical during the _____ stage.

    A. sensorimotor
    B. concrete operations
    C. preoperational
    D. formal operations

38. MOST child development specialists believe that a child's peer groups begin to replace the family as a socializing agent

    A. after the age of 5 or 6
    B. between the age of 2 or 3
    C. near the beginning of adolescence
    D. toward the end of adolescence

39. According to Erik Erikson, a key developmental task for the early elementary school years involves

    A. establishing a personal identity
    B. building confidence, resourcefulness, and enthusiasm
    C. surviving a psychosocial moratorium
    D. handling developmental discontinuity

40. Peter maintains that "everyone else in my class thinks I'm a crook." The mechanism of adjustment Peter is probably utilizing is usually referred to as

    A. projection
    B. rationalization
    C. compensation
    D. identification

41. Of the following, the BEST means of helping a child develop tolerance for tension is to

    A. protect the child from experiencing frustration
    B. make the child face reality through frequent experience of failure
    C. make sure that the child is uniformly successful
    D. help the child achieve some success and face some failure

42. Phil always develops a headache when he is called upon to complete a difficult task. Phil's headache is a(n)

    A. hysteroid reaction
    B. compensatory reaction
    C. reaction formation
    D. paranoid reaction

43. Which of the following is characteristic of the person who overcompensates?

    A. Projection
    B. Repression
    C. Self-repudiation
    D. Rationalization

44. A child who has been rejected by his parents tries to "show off" at every opportunity. Such a child is usually

    A. unaware of the nature of his frustration
    B. not capable of reacting more effectively
    C. reacting objectively to his stress situation
    D. deliberately trying to show his parents his need for affection

45. CHILD-CENTERED GROUP GUIDANCE OF PARENTS as described by Slavson deals with   45.____

    A. the understanding of the behavior and specific acts
    B. of children and ways of dealing with them appropriately
    C. free-associative catharsis which uncovers anxiety-inducing memories, acts and situations
    D. diminution of guilt on the part of the parents
    E. intellectually recognizing and emotionally accepting latent, covert and repressed impulses and strivings in children

46. Which of the following statements BEST expresses the central theme in Bruno Bettelheim's book, LOVE IS NOT ENOUGH? The disturbed child needs to identify with a person who   46.____

    A. accepts his feelings
    B. clearly structures his environment
    C. permits regression
    D. is maternal and "giving"

47. The leisure time activities of the typical pre-adolescent boys' group are mainly given over to   47.____

    A. a succession of activities suited to a changing number of players
    B. games governed by a highly organized series of rules
    C. aimless circulation over a relatively large area looking for something to do
    D. just "hanging around with the boys"

48. The normal age range of reading ability between the best and the poorest reader in a typical sixth grade is about   48.____

    A. 2 years   B. 3 years
    C. 5 years   D. 7 years

49. Of the following books, the one NOT written by A.T. Jersild is   49.____

    A. IN SEARCH OF SELF
    B. CHILDREN'S FEARS
    C. LOVE IS NOT ENOUGH
    D. WHEN TEACHERS FACE THEMSELVES

50. Studies in child development at Yale University were done primarily under the direction of   50.____

    A. Lawrence K. Frank   B. Samuel R. Slavson
    C. Arnold Gesell   D. Albert Deutsch

KEY (CORRECT ANSWERS)

1. B	11. C	21. B	31. C	41. D
2. C	12. D	22. A	32. A	42. A
3. D	13. D	23. C	33. B	43. C
4. C	14. D	24. C	34. B	44. A
5. D	15. B	25. D	35. B	45. A
6. C	16. D	26. B	36. C	46. A
7. B	17. D	27. C	37. D	47. A
8. B	18. B	28. D	38. D	48. D
9. C	19. B	29. C	39. A	49. C
10. A	20. A	30. B	40. A	50. C

EXAMINATION SECTION
TEST 1

DIRECTIONS: Each question or incomplete statement is followed by several suggested answers or completions. Select the one that BEST answers the question or completes the statement. *PRINT THE LETTER OF THE CORRECT ANSWER IN THE SPACE AT THE RIGHT.*

1. It is generally accepted that, of the following, the MOST important medium for developing integration and continuity in learning on the job is
   A. day-to-day experience on the job
   B. the supervisory conference
   C. the staff meeting
   D. the professional seminar

   1.____

2. Assume that you find that one of your workers is over-identifying with a particular client.
   Of the following, the MOST appropriate step for you to take FIRST in dealing with this situation is to
   A. transfer the cases to another worker
   B. inform the worker that he cannot give satisfactory service if he over-identifies with a client
   C. interview the client yourself to determine his feelings about his relationship with the worker
   D. arrange a conference with the worker to discuss the reasons for her over-identification with this client

   2.____

3. The one of the following which is the MOST likely reason why a newly-appointed supervisor would have a tendency to interfere actively in a relationship between one of his workers and a client is that the supervisor
   A. has unresolved feelings about relinquishing the role of worker, and has not yet accepted his role as supervisor
   B. must give direct assistance in the situation because the worker cannot handle it
   C. is attempting to share with his worker the knowledge and skill which he has developed in direct practice
   D. has not realized that immediate responsibility for work with clients has been delegated to others

   3.____

4. A worker who has a tendency to resist authority and supervision can be helped MOST effectively if, of the following, the supervisor
   A. behaves in a strict and impersonal manner so that the worker will accept his authority as a supervisor
   B. modifies the relationship so that he will be less authoritarian and threatening to the worker
   C. gives the worker a simple, matter-of-fact interpretation of the supervisory relationship and has an understanding acceptance of the worker's response
   D. temporarily establishes a peer relationship with the worker in order to overcome his resistance

   4.____

5. Before interviewing a newly-appointed worker for the first time, of the following, it is DESIRABLE for the supervisor to
   A. learn as much as he can about the worker's background and interests in order to eliminate the routine of asking questions and eliciting answers
   B. review the job information to be covered in order to make it easier to be impersonal and keep to the business at hand
   C. send the worker orientation material about the agency and the job and ask him to study it before the interview
   D. review available information about the worker in order to find an area of shared experience to serve as a *taking off* point for getting acquainted

6. In interviewing a new worker, of the following, it is IMPORTANT for the supervisor to
   A. give direction to the progress of the interview and maintain a leadership role throughout
   B. allow the worker to take the initiative in order to give him full scope for freedom of expression
   C. maintain a non-directional approach so that the worker will reveal his true attitudes and feelings
   D. avoid interrupting the worker, even though he seems to want to do all the talking

7. When a new worker, during his first few days, shows such symptoms of insecurity as *stage fright*, helpless immobility, or extreme talkativeness, of the following, it would be MOST helpful for the supervisor to
   A. start the worker out on some activity in which he is relatively secure
   B. ignore the symptoms and allow the worker to *sink or swim* on his own
   C. have a conference with the worker and interpret to him the reasons for his feelings of insecurity
   D. consider the probability that this worker may not be suited for a profession which requires skill in interpersonal relationships

8. Of the following, the MOST desirable method of minimizing workers' dependence on the supervisor and encouraging self-dependence is to
   A. hold group instead of individual supervisory conferences at regular intervals
   B. schedule individual supervisory conferences only in response to the workers' obvious need for guidance
   C. plan for progressive exposure to other opportunities for learning afforded by the agency and the community
   D. allow workers to learn by trial and error rather than by direct supervisory guidance

9. Of the following, it would NOT be appropriate for the supervisor to use early supervisory conferences with the new workers as a means of
   A. giving him direct practical help in order to get going on the job
   B. estimating the level of his native abilities, professional skills and experience
   C. getting clues as to his characteristic ways of learning in a new situation
   D. assessing his potential for future supervisory responsibility

10. Without careful planning by the supervisor for orientation of the new worker, an informal system of orientation by co-workers inevitably develops.
Such an informal system of orientation is USUALLY
    A. *beneficial*, because many new workers learn more readily when instructed by their peers
    B. *harmful*, because informal orientation by an undesignated co-worker can lead a new worker astray instead of helping him
    C. *beneficial*, because assumption by subordinates of responsibility for orientation will free the supervisor for other urgent work
    D. *harmful*, because such informal orientation by a co-worker will tend to destroy the authority of the supervisor

10.____

11. Of the following, the BEST way for a supervisor to assist a subordinate who has unusual work pressures is to
    A. relieve him of some of his cases until the pressures subside
    B. help him to decide which cases should be given the most attention during the period of pressure, and how to provide coverage for less urgent cases
    C. inform him that he must learn to tolerate and adjust to such pressures
    D. point out that he should learn to understand the causes of the pressures, which probably resulted from his own deficiencies

11.____

12. Many supervisors have a tendency to use case records mainly for the purpose of analysis of the workers' skill or evaluation of their performance.
Of the following, a PROBABLE result of this practice is that
    A. workers are likely to tie-in recording with supervisory evaluation of their work, without giving proper emphasis to their importance in improving service to clients
    B. the worker is likely to devote an inordinate amount of time to case records at the expense of his clients
    C. the records are likely to be too lengthy and detailed, limiting their value for other important purposes
    D. the records are likely to be of little value for administrative and research purposes

12.____

13. A common obstacle to adequate recording in a large social work agency is the fact that many workers consider recording to be a time-consuming chore. In order to obtain the cooperation of staff in keeping proper records, of the following, it is MOST important for an agency to provide
    A. indisputable evidence of the intelligent use of records as tools in formulating policy and improving service
    B. a system of checks and controls to assure that workers are preparing adequate and timely records
    C. adequate clerical services and mechanical equipment for recording
    D. sufficient time for recording in the organization of every job

13.____

14. The one of the following which is NOT a purpose of keeping case records in an agency is
    A. planning
    B. research
    C. training
    D. job classification

14.____

4 (#1)

15. When a supervisor is reviewing the records of a worker, of the following, he should plan to read
    A. records of new cases only, following up each interview selectively
    B. the total caseload, in order to determine which aspects of the worker's performance should be examined
    C. those records which the worker has brought to the supervisor's attention because of the need for help
    D. a block of records selected according to the worker's need for help, and some records selected at random

16. The one of the following which is the PRIMARY purpose of the regular staff meeting in an agency is
    A. initiation of action in order to get the agency's work done
    B. staff training and development
    C. program and policy determination
    D. communication of new policies and procedures

17. Of the following, group supervision in an agency is intended as a means of
    A. strengthening the total supervisory process
    B. shifting the focus of supervision from the individual to the group
    C. saving costs in terms of time and manpower
    D. influencing policy through group interaction

18. The supervisor's job brings him closer to such limiting factors in the operation of an agency as faulty administrative structure, shortage of funds and lack of facilities, inadequacies in personnel practices, community pressures, and excessive workload.
    For the supervisor to make a practice of communicating to his subordinates his feelings of frustration about such limitations in the work setting would be
    A. *appropriate*, because the worker will be more understanding of the supervisor's burdens and frustrations
    B. *inappropriate*, because the climate created will block rather than further the purposes of supervision
    C. *appropriate*, because such communication will create a more democratic climate between the worker and the supervisor
    D. *inappropriate*, because the supervisor must support and condone agency policies and practices in the presence of subordinates

19. A suggestion has been made that the teaching and administrative functions of supervision should be separated, so that the supervisor responsible for teaching would not be responsible for evaluation of the same workers.
    The one of the following which is the MOST important reason for this point of view is that
    A. elements that confer on the supervisor a position of authority and power unduly threaten the learning situation
    B. teaching skill and administrative ability do not usually go together

C. a supervisor who has been responsible for training a worker is likely to be prejudiced in his favor
D. performance evaluation and total job accountability should be two separate functions

20. In reviewing a worker's cases in preparation for a periodic evaluation, you note that she has done a uniformly good job with certain types of cases and poor work with other types of cases.
   Of the following, the BEST approach for you to take in this situation is to
   A. bring this to the worker's attention, find out why she favors certain types of clients, and discuss ways in which she can improve her service to all clients
   B. bring this to the worker's attention and suggest that she may need professional counseling, as she seems to be blocked in working with certain types of cases
   C. assign to her mainly those cases which she handles best and transfer the types of cases which she handles poorly to another worker
   D. accept the fact that a worker cannot be expected to give uniformly good service to all clients, and take no further action

20.____

KEY (CORRECT ANSWERS)

1.	B	11.	B
2.	D	12.	A
3.	A	13.	A
4.	C	14.	D
5.	D	15.	D
6.	A	16.	A
7.	A	17.	A
8.	C	18.	B
9.	D	19.	A
10.	B	20.	A

TEST 2

DIRECTIONS: Each question or incomplete statement is followed by several suggested answers or completions. Select the one that BEST answers the question or completes the statement. *PRINT THE LETTER OF THE CORRECT ANSWER IN THE SPACE AT THE RIGHT.*

1. Of the following, the choice of method to be used in the supervisory process should be influenced MOST by the
    A. number and type of cases carried by each worker
    B. emotional maturity of the worker
    C. number of workers supervised and their past experience
    D. subject matter to be learned and the long-range goals of supervision

    1.____

2. In an evaluation conference with a worker, the BEST approach for the supervisor to take is to
    A. help the worker to identify his strengths as a basis for working on his weaknesses
    B. identify the worker's weaknesses and help him overcome them
    C. allow the worker to identify his weaknesses first and then suggest ways of overcoming them
    D. discuss the worker's weaknesses but emphasize his strengths

    2.____

3. Assume that a worker is discouraged about the progress of his work and feels that it is futile to attempt to cope with many of his cases.
   Of the following, it would be BEST for the supervisor to
    A. suggest to the worker that such feelings are inappropriate for a professional worker
    B. tell the worker that he must seek professional help in order to overcome these feelings
    C. reduce the worker's caseload and give him cases that are less complex
    D. review with the worker several of his cases in which there were obvious accomplishments

    3.____

4. The supervisor is responsible for providing the worker with the following means of support, with the EXCEPTION of
    A. interest and advice on his personal problems
    B. instruction on community resources
    C. inspiration for carrying out the work of the agency
    D. understanding his strengths and limitations

    4.____

5. When a worker frequently takes the initiative in asking questions and discussing problems during a supervisory conference, this is PROBABLY an indication that the
    A. supervisor is not sufficiently interested in the work
    B. conference is a positive learning experience for the worker
    C. worker is hostile and resists supervision
    D. supervisor's position of authority is in question

    5.____

6. When a supervisor finds that one of his workers cannot accept criticism, of the following, it would be BEST for the supervisor to
   A. have the worker transferred to another supervisor
   B. warn the worker of disciplinary proceedings unless his attitude changes
   C. have the worker suspended after explaining the reason
   D. explore with the worker his attitude toward authority

7. Of the following, the condition which the inexperienced worker is LEAST likely to be aware of, without the guidance of the supervisor, is
   A. when he is successful in helping a client
   B. when he is not making progress in helping a client
   C. that he has a personal bias toward certain clients
   D. that he feels insecure because of lack of experience

8. The supervisor should provide an inexperienced worker with controls as well as freedom MAINLY because controls will
   A. enable him to set up his own controls sooner
   B. put him in a situation which is closer to the realities of life
   C. help him to use authority in handling a casework problem
   D. give him a feeling of security and lay the foundation for future self-direction

9. A result of the use of summarized case recording by the worker is that it
   A. gives the supervisor more responsibility for selecting cases to discuss in conference
   B. makes more time available for other activities
   C. lowers the morale of many workers
   D. decreases discussion of cases by the worker and the supervisor

10. The distinction between the role of professional workers and the role of auxiliary or sub-professional workers in an agency is based upon the
    A. position within the agency hierarchy
    B. amount of close supervision given
    C. emergent nature of tasks assigned
    D. functions performed

11. Of the following, the MOST important source of learning for the worker should be
    A. departmental directives and professional literature
    B. his co-workers in the agency
    C. the content of in-service training courses
    D. the clients in his caseload

12. A client is MOST likely to feel that he is receiving acceptance and understanding if the social worker
    A. gets detailed information about the client's problem
    B. demonstrates that he realistically understands the client's problem
    C. has an intellectual understanding of the client's problem
    D. offers the client assurance of assistance

13. A client will be MORE encouraged to speak freely about his problems if the worker
    A. avoids asking too many questions
    B. asks leading rather than pointed questions
    C. suggests possible answers
    D. identifies with the client

14. A client would be MOST likely to be able to accept help in a time of crisis and need if the worker
    A. explains agency policy to him
    B. responds immediately to the client's need
    C. explains why help cannot be given immediately
    D. reaches out to help the client establish his rightful claim for assistance

15. It is a generally accepted principle that the worker should interpret for himself what the client is saying, but usually should not pass his interpretation on to the client because the client
    A. will become hostile to the worker
    B. should arrive at his own conclusions at his own pace
    C. must request the interpretation first
    D. usually wants facts, rather than the worker's interpretation

16. In evaluating the client's capacity to cope with his problems, it is MOST important for the worker to assess his ability to
    A. form close relationships
    B. ask for help
    C. express his hostility
    D. verbalize his difficulties

17. When a worker finds that he disagrees strongly with an agency policy, it is DESIRABLE for him to
    A. share his feelings about the policy with his client
    B. understand fully why he has such strong feelings about the policy
    C. refer cases involving the policy to his supervisor
    D. refuse to give help in cases involving the policy

18. Which of the following practices is BEST for a supervisor to use when assigning work to his staff?
    A. Give workers with seniority the most difficult jobs
    B. Assign all unimportant work to the slower workers
    C. Permit each employee to pick the job he prefers
    D. Make assignments based on the workers' abilities

19. In which of the following instances is a supervisor MOST justified in giving commands to people under his supervision?
    When
    A. they delay in following instructions which have been given to them clearly
    B. they become relaxed and slow about work, and he wants to speed up their production
    C. he must direct them in an emergency situation
    D. he is instructing them on jobs that are unfamiliar to them

20. Which of the following supervisory actions or attitudes is MOST likely to result in getting subordinates to try to do as much work as possible for a supervisor?
    He
    A. shows that his most important interest is in schedules and production goals
    B. consistently pressures his staff to get the work out
    C. never fails to let them know he is in charge
    D. considers their abilities and needs while requiring that production goals be met

20.____

KEY (CORRECT ANSWERS)

1.	D	11.	D
2.	A	12.	B
3.	D	13.	D
4.	A	14	D
5.	B	15.	B
6.	D	16.	A
7.	C	17.	B
8.	D	18.	D
9.	B	19.	C
10.	D	20.	D

TEST 3

DIRECTIONS: Each question or incomplete statement is followed by several suggested answers or completions. Select the one that BEST answers the question or completes the statement. *PRINT THE LETTER OF THE CORRECT ANSWER IN THE SPACE AT THE RIGHT.*

1. One of your workers comes to you and complains in an angry manner about your having chosen him for some particular assignment. In your opinion, the subject of the complaint is trivial land unimportant, but it seems to be quite important to your worker.
   The BEST of the following actions for you to take in this situation is to
   A. allow the worker to continue talking until he has calmed down and then explain the reasons for your having chosen him for that particular assignment
   B. warn the worker to moderate his tone of voice at once because he is bordering on insubordination
   C. tell the worker in a friendly tone that he is making a tremendous fuss over an extremely minor matter
   D. point out to the worker that you are his immediate supervisor and that you are running the unit in accordance with official policy

   1.____

2. The one of the following which is the LEAST desirable action for an assistant supervisor to take in disciplining a subordinate for an infraction of the rules is to
   A. caution him against repetition of the infraction, even if it is minor
   B. point out his progress in applying the rules at the same time that you reprimand him
   C. be as specific as possible in reprimanding him for rule infractions
   D. allow a cooling-off period to elapse before reprimanding him

   2.____

3. A training program for workers assigned to the intake section should include actual practice in simulated interviews under simulated conditions.
   The one of the following educational principles which is the CHIEF justification for this statement is that
   A. the workers will remember what they see better and longer than what they read or hear
   B. the workers will learn more effectively by actually doing the act themselves than they would learn from watching others do it
   C. the conduct of simulated interviews once or twice will enable them to cope with the real situation with little difficulty
   D. a training program must employ methods of a practical nature if the workers are to find anything of lasting value in it

   3.____

4. In order for a supervisor to employ the system of democratic leadership in his supervision, it would generally be BEST for him to
   A. allow his subordinates to assist in deciding on methods of work performance and job assignments but only in those areas where decisions have not been made on higher administrative levels

   4.____

2 (#3)

B. allow his subordinates to decide how to do the required work, interposing his authority when work is not completed on schedule or is improperly completed
C. attempt to make assignments of work to individuals only of the type which they enjoy doing
D. maintain control over job assignment and work production, but allow the subordinates to select methods of work and internal conditions of work at democratically conducted staff conferences

5. In a unit in which supervision has been considered quite effective, it has become necessary to press for above-normal production for a limited period to achieve a required goal.
   The one of the following which is a LEAST likely result of this pressure is that
   A. there will be more *griping* by employees
   B. some workers will do both more and better work than has been normal for them
   C. there will be an enhanced feeling of group unity
   D. there will be increased absenteeism

5.____

6. For a supervisor to encourage competitive feelings among his staff is
   A. *advisable*, chiefly because the workers will perform more efficiently when they have proper motivation
   B. *inadvisable*, chiefly because the workers will not perform well under the pressure of competition
   C. *advisable*, chiefly because the workers will have a greater incentive to perform their job properly
   D. *inadvisable*, chiefly because the workers may focus their attention on areas where they excel and neglect other essential aspects of the job

6.____

7. In selecting jobs to be assigned to a new worker, the supervisor should assign those jobs which
   A. give the worker the greatest variety of experience
   B. offer the worker the greatest opportunity to achieve concrete results
   C. present the worker with the greatest stimulation because of their interesting nature
   D. require the least amount of contact with outside agencies

7.____

8. A supervisor should avoid a detailed discussion of a worker-client interview with a new worker before the worker has fully recorded the interview CHIEFLY because such a discussion might
   A. cover matters which are already fully covered and explained in the written record
   B. make the worker forget some important deal learned during the interview
   C. color the recording according to the worker's reaction to his supervisor's opinions
   D. minimize the worker's feeling of having reached a decision independently

8.____

9. Some supervisors encourage their worker to submit a list of their questions about specific jobs or their comments about problems they wish to discuss in advance of the worker-supervisor conference.
   This practice is
   A. *desirable*, chiefly because it helps to stimulate and focus the worker's thinking about his caseload
   B. *undesirable*, chiefly because it will stifle the worker's free expression of his problems and attitudes
   C. *desirable,* chiefly because it will allow the conference to move along more smoothly and quickly
   D. *undesirable*, chiefly because it will restrict the scope of the conference and the variety of jobs discussed

9._____

10. An alert supervisor hears a worker apparently giving the wrong information to a client and immediately reprimands him severely.
    For the supervisor to reprimand the worker at his point is poor CHIEFLY because
    A. instruction must precede correct performance
    B. oral reprimands are less effective than written reprimands
    C. the worker was given no opportunity to explain his reasons for what he did
    D. more effective training can be obtained by discussing the errors with a group of workers

10._____

11. The one of the following circumstances when it would generally be MOST proper for a supervisor to do a job himself rather than to train a subordinate to do the job is when it is
    A. a job which the supervisor enjoys doing and does well
    B. not a very time-consuming job but an important one
    C. difficult to train another to do the job, yet is not difficult for the supervisor to do
    D. unlikely that this or any similar job will have to be done again at any future time

11._____

12. Effective training of subordinates requires that the supervisor understand certain facts about learning and forgetting processes.
    Among these is the fact that people GENERALLY
    A. forget what they learned at a much greater rate during the first day than during subsequent periods
    B. both learn and forget at a relatively constant rate and this rate is dependent upon their general intellectual capacity
    C. learn at a relatively constant rate except for periods of assimilation when the quantity of retained learning decreases while information is becoming firmly fixed in the mind
    D. learn very slowly at first when introduced to a new topic, after which there is a great increase in the rate of learning

12._____

13. It has been suggested that a subordinate who likes his superior will tend to do better work than one who does not.
    According to the MOST widely held current theories of supervision, this suggestion is a
    A. *bad* one, since personal relationships tend to interfere with proper professional relationships
    B. *bad* one, since the strongest motivating factors are fear and uncertainty
    C. *good* one, since liking one's superior is a motivating factor for good work performance
    D. *good* one, since liking one's supervisor is the most important factor in employee performance

14. One factor which might be given consideration in deciding upon the optimum span of control of a supervisor over his immediate subordinates is the position of the supervisor in the hierarchy of the organization.
    It is generally considered proper that the number of subordinates immediately supervised by a higher, upper echelon supervisor _____ the number supervised by lower level supervisors.
    A. is unrelated to and tends to form no pattern with
    B. should be about the same as
    C. should be larger than
    D. should be smaller than

15. The one of the following instances when it is MOST important for an upper level supervisor to follow the chain of command is when he is
    A. communicating decisions   B. communicating information
    C. receiving suggestions   D. seeking information

16. At the end of his probationary period, a supervisor should be considered potentially valuable in his position if he shows
    A. awareness of his areas of strength and weakness, identification with the administration of the department, and ability to learn under supervision
    B. skill in work, supervision, and administration, and a friendly democratic approach to the staff
    C. knowledge of departmental policies and procedures and ability to carry them out, ability to use authority, and ability to direct the work of the staff
    D. an identification with the department, acceptance of responsibility, and ability to give help to the individuals who are to be supervised

17. Good supervision is selective because
    A. it is not necessary to direct all the activities of the person
    B. a supervisor would never have time to know the whole caseload of a worker
    C. workers resent too much help from a supervisor
    D. too much reading is a waste of valuable time

18. An important administrative problem is how precisely to define the limits of authority that is delegated to subordinate supervisors.
Such definition of limits of authority should be
    A. as precise as possible and practicable in all areas
    B. as precise as possible and practicable in areas of function, but should allow considerable flexibility in the area of personnel management
    C. as precise as possible and practicable in the area
    D. of personnel management, but should allow considerable flexibility in the areas of function
    E. in general terms so as to allow considerable flexibility both in the areas of function and in the areas of personnel management

18.____

19. Experts in the field of personnel relations feel that it is generally a bad practice for subordinate employees to become aware of pending or contemplated changes in policy or organizational set-up via the *grapevine* CHIEFLY because
    A. evidence that one or more responsible officials have proved untrustworthy will undermine confidence in the agency
    B. the information disseminated by this method is seldom entirely accurate and generally spreads needless unrest among the subordinate staff
    C. the subordinate staff may conclude that the administration feels the staff cannot be trusted with the true information
    D. the subordinate staff may conclude that the administration lacks the courage to make an unpopular announcement through official channels

19.____

20. Supervision is subject to many interpretations, depending on the area in which it functions.
Of the following, the statement which represents the MOST appropriate meaning of supervision as it is known in social work practice is that it
    A. is a leadership process for the development of new leaders
    B. is an educational and administrative process aimed at teaching personnel the goal of improved service to the client
    C. is an activity aimed chiefly at insuring that workers will adhere to all agency directives
    D. provides the opportunity for administration to secure staff reaction to agency policies

20.____

21. A supervisor may utilize various methods in the supervisory process.
The one of the following upon which sound supervisory practice rests in the selection of supervisory techniques is
    A. an estimate of the worker arrived at through current and past evaluation of performance as well as through worker's participation
    B. the previous supervisor's evaluation and recommendation
    C. the worker's expression of his personal preference for certain types of experience
    D. the amount of time available to supervisor and supervisee

21.____

22. It is the practice of some supervisors, when they believe that it would be desirable for a subordinate to take a particular action in a case, to inform the subordinate of this in the form of a suggestion rather than in the form of a direct order.
In general, this method of getting a subordinate to take the desired action is
   A. *inadvisable*; it may create in the mind of the subordinate the impression that the supervisor is uncertain about the efficacy of her plan and is trying to avoid whatever responsibility she may have in resolving the case
   B. *advisable*; it provides the subordinate with the maximum opportunity to use her own judgment in handling the case
   C. *inadvisable*; it provides the subordinate with no clear-cut direction and, therefore, is likely to leave her with a feeling of uncertainty and frustration
   D. *advisable*; it presents the supervisor's view in a manner which will be most likely to evoke the subordinate's cooperation

23. A veteran supervisor noticed that one of her workers of average ability had begun developing some bad work habits, becoming especially careless in her recordkeeping. After reprimand from the supervisor, the investigator corrected her errors and has been doing satisfactory work since then.
For the supervisor to keep referring to this period of poor work during her weekly conferences with this employee would generally be considered poor personnel practice CHIEFLY because
   A. praise rather than criticism is generally the best method to use in improving the work of an unsatisfactory worker
   B. the supervisor cannot know whether the employee's errors will follow an established pattern
   C. the fault which evoked the original negative criticism no longer exists
   D. this would tend to frustrate the worker by making her strive overly hard to reach a level of productivity which is beyond her ability to achieve

24. Assume that you are now a supervisor in a specific unit. Two experienced investigators in your unit, both of whom do above average work, have for some time not gotten along with each other for personal reasons Their attitude toward one another has suddenly become hostile and noisy disagreement has taken place in the office.
The BEST action for you to take FIRST in this situation is to
   A. transfer one of the two investigators to another unit where contact with the other investigator will be unnecessary
   B. discuss the problem with the two investigators together, insisting that they confide in you and tell you the cause of their mutual antagonism
   C. confer with the two investigators separately, pointing out to each the need to adopt an adult professional attitude with respect to their on-the-job relations
   D. advise the two investigators that should the situation grow worse, disciplinary action will be considered

25. It has long been recognized that relationships exist between worker morale and working conditions.
The one of the following which BEST clarifies these existing relationships is that morale is
    A. affected for better or worse in direct relationship to the magnitude of the changes in working conditions for better or worse
    B. better when working conditions are better
    C. little affected by working conditions so long as the working conditions do not approach the intolerable
    D. more affected by the degree of interest shown in providing good working conditions than by the actual conditions and may, perversely, be highest when working conditions are worst

25._____

KEY (CORRECT ANSWERS)

1.	A	11.	D
2.	D	12.	A
3.	B	13.	C
4.	A	14.	D
5.	D	15.	A
6.	D	16.	D
7.	B	17.	A
8.	C	18.	A
9.	A	19.	B
10.	C	20.	B

21.	A
22.	D
23.	C
24.	C
25.	D

PREPARING WRITTEN MATERIAL

PARAGRAPH REARRANGEMENT
COMMENTARY

The sentences that follow are in scrambled order. You are to rearrange them in proper order and indicate the letter choice containing the correct answer at the space at the right.

Each group of sentences in this section is actually a paragraph presented in scrambled order. Each sentence in the group has a place in that paragraph; no sentence is to be left out. You are to read each group of sentences and decide upon the best order in which to put the sentences so as to form a well-organized paragraph.

The questions in this section measure the ability to solve a problem when all the facts relevant to its solution are not given.

More specifically, certain positions of responsibility and authority require the employee to discover connection between events sometimes, apparently, unrelated. In order to do this, the employee will find it necessary to correctly infer that unspecified events have probably occurred or are likely to occur. This ability becomes especially important when action must be taken on incomplete information.

Accordingly, these questions require competitors to choose among several suggested alternatives, each of which presents a different sequential arrangement of the events. Competitors must choose the MOST logical of the suggested sequences.

In order to do so, they may be required to draw on general knowledge to infer missing concepts or events that are essential to sequencing the given events. Competitors should be careful to infer only what is essential to the sequence. The plausibility of the wrong alternatives will always require the inclusion of unlikely events or of additional chains of events which are NOT essential to sequencing the given events.

It's very important to remember that you are looking for the best of the four possible choices, and that the best choice of all may not even be one of the answers you're given to choose from.

There is no one right way to solve these problems. Many people have found it helpful to first write out the order of the sentences, as they would have arranged them, on their scrap paper before looking at the possible answers. If their optimum answer is there, this can save them some time. If it isn't, this method can still give insight into solving the problem. Others find it most helpful to just go through each of the possible choices, contrasting each as they go along. You should use whatever method feels comfortable and works for you.

While most of these types of questions are not that difficult, we've added a higher percentage of the difficult type, just to give you more practice. Usually there are only one or two questions on this section that contain such subtle distinctions that you're unable to answer confidently. And you then may find yourself stuck deciding between two possible choices, neither of which you're sure about.

EXAMINATION SECTION
TEST 1

DIRECTIONS: Each group of sentences in this section is actually a paragraph presented in scrambled order. Each sentence in the group has a place in that paragraph; no sentence is to be left out. You are to read each group of sentences, so as to form a well-organized paragraph. Before trying to answer the questions which follow each group of sentences, jot down the correct order of the sentences. Then answer each of the questions by printing the letter of the correct answer in the space at the right. Remember that you will receive credit only for answers marked.

P. The infant only feels the positive stimulation of warmth and food and does not differentiate the warmth and food from their source, mother.
Q. The infant, at the moment of birth, would feel the fear of dying if gracious fate did not preserve it from any awareness of the anxiety involved in the separation from mother.
R. The infant's state, then, is what has been called narcissism.
S. Mother is warmth, mother is food, mother is the euphoric state of satisfaction and security.
T. Even after being born, the infant is not yet aware of itself, and of the world as being outside of itself.

1. Which sentence did you put before Sentence Q?

   A. P
   B. R
   C. S
   D. T
   E. None of the above. Sentence Q is first.

2. Which sentence did you put after Sentence S?

   A. P
   B. Q
   C. R
   D. T
   E. None of the above. Sentence S is last.

3. Which sentence did you put before Sentence P?

   A. Q
   B. R
   C. S
   D. T
   E. None of the above. Sentence P is first.

4. Which sentence did you put after Sentence P?

   A. Q
   B. R
   C. S
   D. T
   E. None of the above. Sentence P is last.

5. Which sentence did you put after Sentence R?

   A. P
   B. Q
   C. S
   D. T
   E. None of the above. Sentence R is last.

KEY (CORRECT ANSWERS)

1. E
2. C
3. D
4. C
5. E

TEST 2

DIRECTIONS: Each group of sentences in this section is actually a paragraph presented in scrambled order. Each sentence in the group has a place in that paragraph; no sentence is to be left out. You are to read each group of sentences, so as to form a well-organized paragraph. Before trying to answer the questions which follow each group of sentences, jot down the correct order of the sentences. Then answer each of the questions by printing the letter of the correct answer in the space at the right. Remember that you will receive credit only for answers marked.

P. Then it requires knowledge and effort.
Q. The former is my view.
R. Or is love a pleasant sensation, something one *falls into* if one is lucky?
S. The majority of people today, however, believe in the latter.
T. Is love an art?

1. Which sentence did you put second?

   A. P   B. Q   C. R   D. S   E. T

2. Which sentence did you put after Sentence S?

   A. P
   B. Q
   C. R
   D. T
   E. None of the above. Sentence S is last.

3. Which sentence did you put before Sentence Q?

   A. P
   B. R
   C. S
   D. T
   E. None of the above. Sentence Q is first.

4. Which sentence did you put before Sentence P?

   A. Q
   B. R
   C. S
   D. T
   E. None of the above. Sentence P is first.

5. Which sentence did you put after Sentence Q?

   A. P
   B. R
   C. S
   D. T
   E. None of the above. Sentence Q is last.

KEY (CORRECT ANSWERS)

1. A
2. E
3. B
4. D
5. C

TEST 3

DIRECTIONS: Each group of sentences in this section is actually a paragraph presented in scrambled order. Each sentence in the group has a place in that paragraph; no sentence is to be left out. You are to read each group of sentences, so as to form a well-organized paragraph. Before trying to answer the questions which follow each group of sentences, jot down the correct order of the sentences. Then answer each of the questions by printing the letter of the correct answer in the space at the right. Remember that you will receive credit only for answers marked.

P. Indeed, in his time, Freud's theories of sex had a challenging and revolutionary character.
Q. Sexual mores have changed so much that Freud's theories no longer are shocking to the middle classes.
R. Freud has been criticized for his overevaluation of sex.
S. But what was true sixty years ago is no longer true.
T. This criticism resulted from a wish to remove an element from Freud's system which might arouse criticism among conventionally-minded people.

1. Which sentence did you put last?
   A. P   B. Q   C. R   D. S   E. T

2. Which sentence did you put before Sentence Q?
   A. P
   B. R
   C. S
   D. T
   E. None of the above. Sentence Q is first.

3. Which sentence did you put after Sentence T?
   A. P
   B. Q
   C. R
   D. S
   E. None of the above. Sentence T is last.

4. Which sentence did you put before Sentence R?
   A. P
   B. Q
   C. S
   D. T
   E. None of the above. Sentence R is first.

5. Which sentence did you put after Sentence R?
   A. P
   B. Q
   C. S
   D. T
   E. None of the above. Sentence R is last.

KEY (CORRECT ANSWERS)

1. B
2. C
3. A
4. E
5. D

TEST 4

DIRECTIONS: Each group of sentences in this section is actually a paragraph presented in scrambled order. Each sentence in the group has a place in that paragraph; no sentence is to be left out. You are to read each group of sentences, so as to form a well-organized paragraph. Before trying to answer the questions which follow each group of sentences, jot down the correct order of the sentences. Then answer each of the questions by printing the letter of the correct answer in the space at the right. Remember that you will receive credit only for answers marked.

P. Early Scandanavian accounts, as well, are too mythological and legendary to serve as history.
Q. The first trustworthy written evidence of a kingdom of Denmark belongs to the beginning of the Viking period.
R. Ancient Roman knowledge of this remote country was fragmentary and unreliable.
S. Archaeology and the study of place names, however, provide a certain amount of information about the earliest settlements.
T. Everything before that is prehistory.

1. Which sentence did you put fourth?
   A. P   B. B. Q   C. C. R   D. D. S   E. E. T

2. Which sentence did you put after Sentence T?
   A. Q
   B. R
   C. S
   D. None of the above. Sentence T is last.

3. Which sentence did you put after Sentence Q?
   A. P
   B. R
   C. S
   D. T
   E. None of the above. Sentence Q is last.

4. Which sentence did you put before Sentence Q?
   A. P
   B. R
   C. S
   D. T
   E. None of the above. Sentence Q is first.

5. Which sentence did you put after Sentence P?
   A. Q
   B. R
   C. S
   D. T
   E. None of the above. Sentence P is last.

KEY (CORRECT ANSWERS)

1. A
2. C
3. D
4. E
5. C

TEST 5

DIRECTIONS: Each group of sentences in this section is actually a paragraph presented in scrambled order. Each sentence in the group has a place in that paragraph; no sentence is to be left out. You are to read each group of sentences, so as to form a well-organized paragraph. Before trying to answer the questions which follow each group of sentences, jot down the correct order of the sentences. Then answer each of the questions by printing the letter of the correct answer in the space at the right. Remember that you will receive credit only for answers marked.

P. In 1268, ambassadors were required to surrender all gifts they had received on their missions.
Q. In the 13th century, the Venetian republic began to lay down rules of conduct for its ambassadors.
R. In 1288, it was decreed that ambassadors were to report in writing on the results of their missions.
S. Such reports are a mine of historical material.
T. It is in Venice that the origins of modern diplomacy are to be sought.

1. Which sentence did you put second?
   A. P   B. Q   C. R   D. S   E. T

2. Which sentence did you put after Sentence R?
   A. P
   B. Q
   C. S
   D. T
   E. None of the above. Sentence R is last.

3. Which sentence did you put before Sentence P?
   A. Q
   B. R
   C. S
   D. T
   E. None of the above. Sentence P is first.

4. Which sentence did you put before Sentence T?
   A. P
   B. Q
   C. R
   D. S
   E. None of the above. Sentence T is first.

5. Which sentence did you put last?
   A. P   B. B. Q   C. C. R   D. D. S   E. E. T

KEY (CORRECT ANSWERS)

1. B
2. C
3. A
4. E
5. D

EXAMINATION SECTION
TEST 1

DIRECTIONS: Each group of sentences in this section is actually a paragraph presented in scrambled order. Each sentence in the group has a place in that paragraph; no sentence is to be left out. You are to read each group of sentences, so as to form a well-organized paragraph. Before trying to answer the questions which follow each group of sentences, jot down the correct order of the sentences. Then answer each of the questions by printing the letter of the correct answer in the space at the right. Remember that you will receive credit only for answers marked.

P. American divorce statutes derive principally from ecclesiastical law and embody certain moral concepts.
Q. Divorces are granted under such statutes only to an innocent spouse where the other spouse has been guilty of statutorily-defined misconduct.
R. All the states and territories of the United States grant divorces.
S. If, therefore, both parties are guilty, there can be no divorce.
T. The statutes of each territory and state determine the permissible grounds for the divorces granted in that territory and state.

1. Which sentence did you put after Sentence R?

    A. P
    B. Q
    C. S
    D. T
    E. None of the above. Sentence R is last.

2. Which sentence did you put before Sentence Q?

    A. P
    B. R
    C. S
    D. T
    E. None of the above. Sentence Q is first.

3. Which sentence did you put after Sentence S?

    A. P
    B. Q
    C. R
    D. T
    E. None of the above. Sentence S is last.

4. Which sentence did you put last?

    A. P   B. Q   C. R   D. S   E. T

5. Which sentence did you put before Sentence R? 5.____

    A. P
    B. Q
    C. S
    D. T
    E. None of the above. Sentence R is first.

KEY (CORRECT ANSWERS)

1. D
2. A
3. E
4. D
5. E

TEST 2

DIRECTIONS: Each group of sentences in this section is actually a paragraph presented in scrambled order. Each sentence in the group has a place in that paragraph; no sentence is to be left out. You are to read each group of sentences, so as to form a well-organized paragraph. Before trying to answer the questions which follow each group of sentences, jot down the correct order of the sentences. Then answer each of the questions by printing the letter of the correct answer in the space at the right. Remember that you will receive credit only for answers marked.

P. Sporting dogs include pointers, setters, and retrievers.
Q. Terriers include airedales, fox terriers, and schnauzers.
R. Hounds include bloodhounds, greyhounds, and wolfhounds.
S. Working dogs include collies, sheep dogs, and boxers.
T. Four of the major classifications of dogs are sporting dogs, hounds, terriers, and working dogs.

1. Which sentence did you put before Sentence R?
   A. P
   B. Q
   C. S
   D. T
   E. None of the above. Sentence R is first.

2. Which sentence did you put after Sentence S?
   A. P
   B. Q
   C. R
   D. T
   E. None of the above. Sentence S is last.

3. Which sentence did you put before Sentence Q?
   A. P
   B. R
   C. S
   D. T
   E. None of the above. Sentence Q is first.

4. Which sentence did you put last?
   A. P   B. Q   C. R   D. S   E. T

5. Which sentence did you put after Sentence T?
   A. P
   B. Q
   C. R
   D. S
   E. None of the above. Sentence T is last.

KEY (CORRECT ANSWERS)

1. A
2. E
3. B
4. D
5. A

TEST 3

DIRECTIONS: Each group of sentences in this section is actually a paragraph presented in scrambled order. Each sentence in the group has a place in that paragraph; no sentence is to be left out. You are to read each group of sentences, so as to form a well-organized paragraph. Before trying to answer the questions which follow each group of sentences, jot down the correct order of the sentences. Then answer each of the questions by printing the letter of the correct answer in the space at the right. Remember that you will receive credit only for answers marked.

P. Dostoevsky came to be regarded as the most promising of Russia's young novelists.
Q. He continued, however, to write prolifically for the next three years, producing three novels in that period.
R. Unlike his later works, too, they betray intense interest in problems of form and show originality of verbal expression.
S. But his second novel, THE DOUBLE, disappointed critics, and his success began to wane.
T. These early works display the strong influence of Gogol.

1. Which sentence did you put before Sentence P?   1.____

   A. Q
   B. R
   C. S
   D. T
   E. None of the above. Sentence P is first.

2. Which sentence did you put third?   2.____

   A. P   B. Q   C. R   D. S   E. T

3. Which sentence did you put after Sentence Q?   3.____

   A. P
   B. R
   C. S
   D. T
   E. None of the above. Sentence Q is last.

4. Which sentence did you put last?   4.____

   A. P   B. Q   C. R   D. S   E. T

5. Which sentence did you put before Sentence S?   5.____

   A. P
   B. Q
   C. R
   D. T
   E. None of the above. Sentence S is first.

KEY (CORRECT ANSWERS)

1. E
2. B
3. D
4. C
5. A

TEST 4

DIRECTIONS: Each group of sentences in this section is actually a paragraph presented in scrambled order. Each sentence in the group has a place in that paragraph; no sentence is to be left out. You are to read each group of sentences, so as to form a well-organized paragraph. Before trying to answer the questions which follow each group of sentences, jot down the correct order of the sentences. Then answer each of the questions by printing the letter of the correct answer in the space at the right. Remember that you will receive credit only for answers marked.

P. Not every state of awareness in sleep is classifiable as a dream state.
Q. Dreams are ordinarily defined as states of consciousness taking place during sleep.
R. For example, people often hear a telephone ringing while asleep, and awaken to find that a telephone is, indeed, ringing.
S. And sleep is not invariably necessary to the manifestation of dream consciousness.
T. This definition is hardly adequate.

1. Which sentence did you put after Sentence T?
   A. P
   B. Q
   C. R
   D. S
   E. None of the above. Sentence T is last.

2. Which sentence did you put after Sentence R?
   A. P
   B. Q
   C. S
   D. T
   E. None of the above. Sentence R is last.

3. Which sentence did you put after Sentence Q?
   A. P
   B. R
   C. S
   D. T
   E. None of the above. Sentence Q is last.

4. Which sentence did you put after Sentence P?
   A. Q
   B. R
   C. S
   D. T
   E. None of the above. Sentence P is last.

5. Which sentence did you put before Sentence Q?

   A. P
   B. R
   C. S
   D. T
   E. None of the above. Sentence Q is first.

5.____

KEY (CORRECT ANSWERS)

1. A
2. C
3. D
4. B
5. E

TEST 5

DIRECTIONS: Each group of sentences in this section is actually a paragraph presented in scrambled order. Each sentence in the group has a place in that paragraph; no sentence is to be left out. You are to read each group of sentences, so as to form a well-organized paragraph. Before trying to answer the questions which follow each group of sentences, jot down the correct order of the sentences. Then answer each of the questions by printing the letter of the correct answer in the space at the right. Remember that you will receive credit only for answers marked.

P. Yet the long history of disarmament proposals and counterproposals is discouraging.
Q. It is also a wasteful mode of international competition.
R. Only those, therefore, who despair of the West's ability to compete constructively put their trust in the arms race.
S. It is now generally accepted that the arms race is too dangerous for any nation to continue pursuing without restraint or inhibition.
T. The fears and tensions it generates prevent East and West from competing constructively.

1. Which sentence did you put next to last?
   A. P   B. Q   C. R   D. S   E. T

2. Which sentence did you put before Sentence T?
   A. P
   B. Q
   C. R
   D. S
   E. None of the above. Sentence T is first.

3. Which sentence did you put before Sentence Q?
   A. P
   B. R
   C. S
   D. T
   E. None of the above. Sentence Q is first.

4. Which sentence did you put after Sentence R?
   A. P
   B. Q
   C. S
   D. T
   E. None of the above. Sentence R is last.

5. Which sentence did you put before Sentence S?

    A. P
    B. Q
    C. R
    D. T
    E. None of the above. Sentence S is first.

KEY (CORRECT ANSWERS)

1. C
2. B
3. C
4. A
5. E

PREPARING WRITTEN MATERIAL
EXAMINATION SECTION
TEST 1

DIRECTIONS: Each of Questions 1 through 5 consists of a sentence which may or may not be an example of good formal English usage. Examine each sentence, considering grammar, punctuation, spelling, capitalization, and awkwardness. Then choose the correct statement about it from the four options below it. If the English usage in the sentence given is better than any of the changes suggested in options B, C, or D, pick option A. (Do not pick an option that will change the meaning of the sentence.) *PRINT THE LETTER OF THE CORRECT ANSWER IN THE SPACE AT THE RIGHT.*

1. I don't know who could possibly of broken it. 1.____
    A. This is an example of good formal English usage.
    B. The word "who" should be replaced by the word "whom."
    C. The word "of" should be replaced by the word "have."
    D. The word "broken" should be replaced by the word "broke."

2. Telephoning is easier than to write. 2.____
    A. This is an example of good formal English usage.
    B. The word "telephoning" should be spelled "telephoneing."
    C. The word "than" should be replaced by the word "then."
    D. The words "to write" should be replaced by the word "writing."

3. The two operators who have been assigned to these consoles are on vacation. 3.____
    A. This is an example of good formal English usage.
    B. A comma should be placed after the word "operators."
    C. The word "who" should be replaced by the word "whom."
    D. The word "are" should be replaced by the word "is."

4. You were suppose to teach me how to operate a plugboard. 4.____
    A. This is an example of good formal English usage.
    B. The word "were" should be replaced by the word "was."
    C. The word "suppose" should be replaced by the word "supposed."
    D. The word "teach" should be replaced by the word "learn."

5. If you had taken my advice; you would have spoken with him. 5.____
    A. This is an example of good formal English usage.
    B. The word "advice" should be spelled "advise."
    C. The words "had taken" should be replaced by the word "take."
    D. The semicolon should be changed to a comma.

KEY (CORRECT ANSWERS)

1. C
2. D
3. A
4. C
5. D

TEST 2

DIRECTIONS: Select the correct answer. *PRINT THE LETTER OF THE CORRECT ANSWER IN THE SPACE AT THE RIGHT.*

1. The one of the following sentences which is MOST acceptable from the viewpoint of correct grammatical usage is:
    A. I do not know which action will have worser results.
    B. He should of known better.
    C. Both the officer on the scene, and his immediate supervisor, is charged with the responsibility.
    D. An officer must have initiative because his supervisor will not always be available to answer questions.

    1.____

2. The one of the following sentences which is MOST acceptable from the viewpoint of correct grammatical usage is:
    A. Of all the officers available, the better one for the job will be picked.
    B. Strict orders were given to all the officers, except he.
    C. Study of the law will enable you to perform your duties more efficiently.
    D. It seems to me that you was wrong in failing to search the two men.

    2.____

3. The one of the following sentences which does NOT contain a misspelled word is:
    A. The duties you will perform are similar to the duties of a patrolman.
    B. Officers must be constantly alert to sieze the initiative.
    C. Officers in this organization are not entitled to special privileges.
    D. Any changes in procedure will be announced publically.

    3.____

4. The one of the following sentences which does NOT contain a misspelled word is:
    A. It will be to your advantage to keep your firearm in good working condition.
    B. There are approximately fourty men on sick leave.
    C. Your first duty will be to pursuade the person to obey the law.
    D. Fires often begin in flameable material kept in lockers.

    4.____

5. The one of the following sentences which does NOT contain a misspelled word is:
    A. Offices are not required to perform technical maintainance.
    B. He violated the regulations on two occasions.
    C. Every employee will be held responable for errors.
    D. This was his nineth absence in a year.

    5.____

KEY (CORRECT ANSWERS)

1. D
2. C
3. C
4. A
5. B

TEST 3

DIRECTIONS: Select the correct answer. *PRINT THE LETTER OF THE CORRECT ANSWER IN THE SPACE AT THE RIGHT.*

1. You are answering a letter that was written on the letterhead of the ABC Company and signed by James H. Wood, Treasurer.
   What is usually considered to be the correct salutation to use in your reply?
   A. Dear ABC Company:
   B. Dear Sirs:
   C. Dear Mr. Wood:
   D. Dear Mr. Treasurer:

   1.____

2. Assume that one of your duties is to handle routine letters of inquiry from the public.
   The one of the following which is usually considered to be MOST desirable in replying to such a letter is a
   A. detailed answer handwritten on the original letter of inquiry
   B. phone call, since you can cover details more easily over the phone than in a letter
   C. short letter giving the specific information requested
   D. long letter discussing all possible aspects of the question raised

   2.____

3. The CHIEF reason for dividing a letter into paragraphs is to
   A. make the message clear to the reader by starting a new paragraph for each new topic
   B. make a short letter occupy as much of the page as possible
   C. keep the reader's attention by providing a pause from time to time
   D. make the letter look neat and businesslike

   3.____

4. Your superior has asked you to send an e-mail from your agency to a government agency in another city. He has written out the message and has indicated the name of the government agency.
   When you dictate the message to your secretary, which of the following items that your superior has NOT mentioned must you be sure to include?
   A. Today's date
   B. The full address of the government agency
   C. A polite opening such as "Dear Sirs"
   D. A final sentence such as "We would appreciate hearing from your agency in reply as soon as is convenient for you"

   4.____

5. The one of the following sentences which is grammatically preferable to the others is:
   A. Our engineers will go over your blueprints so that you may have no problems in construction.
   B. For a long time he had been arguing that we, not he, are to blame for the confusion.
   C. I worked on this automobile for two hours and still cannot find out what is wrong with it.
   D. Accustomed to all kinds of hardships, fatigue seldom bothers veteran policemen.

   5.____

KEY (CORRECT ANSWERS)

1. C
2. C
3. A
4. B
5. A

TEST 4

DIRECTIONS: Select the correct answer. *PRINT THE LETTER OF THE CORRECT ANSWER IN THE SPACE AT THE RIGHT.*

1. Suppose that an applicant for a job as snow laborer presents a letter from a former employer stating: "John Smith has a pleasing manner and never got into an argument with his fellow employees. He was never late or absent." This letter
    A. indicates that with some training Smith will make a good snow gang boss
    B. presents no definite evidence of Smith's ability to do snow work
    C. proves definitely that Smith has never done any snow work before
    D. proves definitely that Smith will do better than average work as a snow laborer

    1.____

2. Suppose you must write a letter to a local organization in your section refusing a request in connection with collection of their refuse.
   You should start the letter by
    A. explaining in detail the consideration you gave the request
    B. praising the organization for its service to the community
    C. quoting the regulation which forbids granting the request
    D. stating your regret that the request cannot be granted

    2.____

3. Suppose a citizen writes in for information as to whether or not he may sweep refuse into the gutter. A Sanitation officer answers as follows:
   Dear Sir:
      No person is permitted to litter, sweep, throw or cast, or direct, suffer or permit any person under his control to litter, sweep, throw or cast any ashes, garbage, paper, dust, or other rubbish or refuse into any public street or place, vacant lot, air shaft, areaway, backyard or court.
                           Very truly yours,
                           John Doe
   This letter is *poorly* written CHIEFLY because
    A. the opening is not indented   B. the thought is not clear
    C. the tone is too formal and cold   D. there are too many commas used

    3.____

4. A section of a disciplinary report written by a Sanitation officer states: "It is requested that subject Sanitation man be advised that his future activities be directed towards reducing his recurrent tardiness else disciplinary action will be initiated which may result in summary discharge."
   This section of the report is *poorly* written MAINLY because
    A. at least one word is misspelled   B. it is not simply expressed
    C. more than one idea is expressed   D. the purpose is not stated

    4.____

5. A section of a disciplinary report written by an officer states: "He comes in late. He takes too much time for lunch. He is lazy. I recommend his services be dispensed with."
   This section of the report is *poorly* written MAINLY because
    A. it ends with a preposition   B. it is not well organized
    C. no supporting facts are stated   D. the sentences are too simple

    5.____

111

KEY (CORRECT ANSWERS)

1. B
2. D
3. C
4. B
5. C

PREPARING WRITTEN MATERIALS
EXAMINATION SECTION
TEST 1

DIRECTIONS: Each question or incomplete statement is followed by several suggested answers or completions. Select the one that BEST answers the question or completes the statement. *PRINT THE LETTER OF THE CORRECT ANSWER IN THE SPACE AT THE RIGHT.*

Questions 1-21.

DIRECTIONS: In each of the following sentences, which were taken from students' transcripts, there may be an error. Indicate the appropriate correction in the space at the right. If the sentence is correct as is, indicate this choice. Unnecessary changes will be considered incorrect.

1. In that building there seemed to be representatives of Teachers College, the Veterans Bureau, and the Businessmen's Association. 1.____
   A. Teacher's College
   B. Veterans' Bureau
   C. Businessmens Association
   D. Correct as is

2. In his travels, he visited St. Paul, San Francisco, Springfield, Ohio, and Washington, D.C. 2.____
   A. Ohio and
   B. Saint Paul
   C. Washington, D.C.
   D. Correct as is

3. As a result of their purchasing a controlling interest in the syndicate, it was well-known that the Bureau of Labor Statistics' calculations would be unimportant. 3.____
   A. of them purchasing
   B. well known
   C. Statistics
   D. Correct as is

4. Walter Scott, Jr.'s, attempt to emulate his father's success was doomed to failure. 4.____
   A. Junior's,
   B. Scott's, Jr.
   C. Scott, Jr.'s attempt
   D. Correct as is

5. About B.C. 250 the Romans invaded Great Britain, and remains of their highly developed civilization can still be seen. 5.____
   A. 250 B.C.
   B. Britain and
   C. highly-developed
   D. Correct as is

6. The two boss's sons visited the children's department. 6.____
   A. bosses
   B. bosses'
   C. childrens'
   D. Correct as is

7. Miss Amex not only approved the report, but also decided that it needed no revision.
   A. report; but
   B. report but
   C. report. But
   D. Correct as is

   7._____

8. Here's brain food in a jiffy—economical, too!
   A. economical too!
   B. "brain food"
   C. jiffy-economical
   D. Correct as is

   8._____

9. She said, "He likes the "Gatsby Look" very much."
   A. said "He
   B. "he
   C. 'Gatsby Look'
   D. Correct as is

   9._____

10. We anticipate that we will be able to visit them briefly in Los Angeles on Wednesday after a five day visit.
    A. Wednes-
    B. 5 day
    C. five-day
    D. Correct as is

    10._____

11. She passed all her tests, and, she now has a good position.
    A. tests, and she
    B. past
    C. tests;
    D. Correct as is

    11._____

12. The billing clerk said, "I will send the bill today"; however, that was a week ago, and it hasn't arrived yet!
    A. today;"
    B. today,"
    C. ago and
    D. Correct as is

    12._____

13. "She types at more-than-average speed," Miss Smith said, "but I feel that it is a result of marvelous concentration and self control on her part."
    A. more than average
    B. "But
    C. self-control
    D. Correct as is

    13._____

14. The state of Alaska, the largest state in the union, is also the northernmost state.
    A. Union
    B. Northernmost State
    C. State of Alaska
    D. Correct as is

    14._____

15. The memoirs of Ex-President Nixon, according to figures, sold more copies than <u>Six Crises</u>, the book he wrote in the '60s.
    A. Six Crises
    B. ex-President
    C. 60s
    D. Correct as is

    15._____

16. "There are three principal elements, determining the hazard of buildings: the contents hazard, the fire resistance of the structure, and the character of the interior finish," concluded the speaker.
    The one of the following statements that is MOST acceptable is that, in the above passage,
    A. the comma following the word *elements* is incorrect
    B. the colon following the word *buildings* is incorrect
    C. the comma following the word *finish* is incorrect
    D. there is no error in the punctuation of the sentence

    16._____

17. He spoke on his favorite topic, "Why We Will Win." (How could I stop him?) 17.____
 A. Win". B. him?). C. him)? C. Correct as is

18. "All any insurance policy is, is a contract for services," said my insurance 18.____
 agent, Mr. Newton.
 A. Insurance Policy B. Insurance Agent
 C. policy is is a D. Correct as is

19. Inasmuch as the price list has now been up dated, we should sent it to the 19.____
 printer.
 A. In as much B. updated
 C. pricelist D. Correct as is

20. We feel that "Our know-how" is responsible for the improvement in technical 20.____
 developments.
 A. "our B. know how C. that, D. Correct as is

21. Did Cortez conquer the Incas? the Aztecs? the South American Indians? 21.____
 A. Incas, the Aztecs, the South American Indians?
 B. Incas; the Aztecs; the South American Indians?
 C. south American Indians?
 D. Correct as is

22. Which one of the following forms for the typed name of the dictator in the closing 22.____
 lines of a letter is generally MOST acceptable in the United States?
 A. (Dr.) James F. Farley B. Dr. James F. Farley
 C. Me. James J. Farley, Ph.D. D. James F. Farley

23. The plural of 23.____
 A. turkey is turkies B. cargo is cargoes
 C. bankruptcy is bankruptcys D. son-in-law is son-in-laws

24. The abbreviation viz. means MOST NEARLY 24.____
 A. namely B. for example
 C. the following D. see

25. In the sentence, *A man in a light-gray suit waited thirty-five minutes in the* 25.____
 ante-room for the all-important document, the word IMPROPERLY hyphenated
 is
 A. light-gray B. thirty-five C. ante-room D. all-important

KEY (CORRECT ANSWERS)

1.	D	11.	A
2.	C	12.	D
3.	B	13.	D
4.	D	14.	A
5.	A	15.	B
6.	B	16.	A
7.	B	17.	D
8.	D	18.	D
9.	C	19.	B
10.	C	20.	A

21. D
22. D
23. B
24. A
25. C

TEST 2

DIRECTIONS: Each question or incomplete statement is followed by several suggested answers or completions. Select the one that BEST answers the question or completes the statement. *PRINT THE LETTER OF THE CORRECT ANSWER IN THE SPACE AT THE RIGHT.*

Questions 1-10.

DIRECTIONS: In each of the following groups of four sentences, one sentence contains an error in sentence structure, grammar, usage, diction, or punctuation. Indicate the INCORRECT sentence.

1. A. The lecture finished, the audience began asking questions. 1.____
    B. Any man who could accomplish that task the world would regard as a hero.
    C. Our respect and admiration are mutual.
    D. George did like his mother told him, despite the importunities of his playmates.

2. A. I cannot but help admiring you for your dedication to your job. 2.____
    B. Because they had insisted upon showing us films of their travels, we have lost many friends whom we once cherished.
    C. I am constrained to admit that your remarks made me feel bad.
    D. My brother having been notified of his acceptance by the university of his choice, my father immediately made plans for a vacation.

3. A. In no other country is freedom of speech and assembly so jealously guarded. 3.____
    B. Being a beatnik, he felt that it would be a betrayal of his cause to wear shoes and socks at the same time.
    C. Riding over the Brooklyn Bridge gave us an opportunity to see the Manhattan skyline.
    D. In 1961, flaunting SEATO, the North Vietnamese crossed the line of demarcation.

4. A. I have enjoyed the study of the Spanish language not only because of its beauty and the opportunity it offers to understand the Hispanic culture but also to make use of it in the business associations I have in South America. 4.____
    B. The opinions he expressed were decidedly different from those he had held in his youth.
    C. Had he actually studied, he certainly would have passed.
    D. A supervisor should be patient, tactful, and firm.

5. A. At this point we were faced with only three alternatives: to push on, to remain where we were, or to return to the village. 5.____
    B. We had no choice but to forgive so venial a sin.
    C. In their new picture, the Warners are flouting tradition.
    D. Photographs taken revealed that 2.5 square miles had been burned.

117

6. A. He asked whether he might write to his friends.
    B. There are many problems which must be solved before we can be assured of world peace.
    C. Each person with whom I talked expressed his opinion freely.
    D. Holding on to my saddle with all my strength the horse galloped down the road at a terrifying pace.

7. A. After graduating high school, he obtained a position as a runner in Wall Street.
    B. Last night, in a radio address, the President urged us to subscribe to the Red Cross.
    C. In the evening, light spring rain cooled the streets.
    D. "Un-American" is a word which has been used even by those whose sympathies may well have been pro-Nazi.

8. A. It is hard to conceive of their not doing good work.
    B. Who won—you or I?
    C. He having read the speech caused much comment.
    D. Their finishing the work proves that it can be done.

9. A. Our course of study should not be different now than it was five years ago.
    B. I cannot deny myself the pleasure of publicly thanking the mayor for his actions.
    C. The article on "Morale" has appeared in the Times Literary Supplement.
    D. He died of tuberculosis contracted during service with the Allied Forces.

10. A. If it wasn't for a lucky accident, he would still be an office-clerk.
    B. It is evident that teachers need help.
    C. Rolls of postage stamps may be bought at stationery stores.
    D. Addressing machines are used by firms that publish magazines.

11. The one of the following sentences which contains NO error in usage is:
    A. After the robbers left, the proprietor stood tied in his chair for about two hours before help arrived.
    B. In the cellar I found the watchmans' hat and coat.
    C. The persons living in adjacent apartments stated that they had heard no unusual noises.
    D. Neither a knife or any firearms were found in the room.

12. The one of the following sentences which contains NO error in usage is:
    A. The policeman lay a firm hand on the suspect's shoulder.
    B. It is true that neither strength nor agility are the most important requirement for a good patrolman.
    C. Good citizens constantly strive to do more than merely comply the restraints imposed by society.
    D. Twenty years is considered a severe sentence for a felony.

13. Select the sentence containing an adverbial objective. 13.____
    A. Concepts can only acquire content when they are connected, however indirectly, with sensible experience.
    B. The cloth was several shades too light to match the skirt which she had discarded.
    C. The Gargantuan Hall of Commons became a tri-daily horror to Kurt, because two youths discerned that he had a beard and courageously told the world about it.
    D. Brooding morbidly over the event, Elsie found herself incapable of engaging in normal activity.

14. Select the sentence containing a verb in the subjunctive mood. 14.____
    A. Had he known of the new experiments with penicillin dust for the cure of colds, he might have been tempted to try them in his own office.
    B. I should be very much honored by your visit.
    C. Though he has one of the highest intelligence quotients in his group, he seems far below the average in actual achievement.
    D. Long had I known that he would be the man finally selected for such signal honors.

15. Select the sentence containing one (or more) passive perfect participle(s). 15.____
    A. Having been apprised of the consequences of his refusal to answer, the witness finally revealed the source of his information.
    B. To have been placed in such an uncomfortable position was perhaps unfair to a journalist of his reputation.
    C. When deprived of special immunity he had, of course, no alternative but to speak.
    D. Having been obdurate until now, he was reluctant to surrender under this final pressure exerted upon him.

16. Select the sentence containing a predicate nominative. 16.____
    A. His dying wish, which he expressed almost with his last breath, was to see that justice was done toward his estranged wife.
    B. So long as we continue to elect our officials in truly democratic fashion, we shall have the power to preserve our liberties.
    C. We could do nothing, at this juncture, but walk the five miles back to camp.
    D. There was the spaniel, wet and cold and miserable, waiting silently at the door.

17. Select the sentence containing exactly TWO adverbs. 17.____
    A. The gentlemen advanced with exasperating deliberateness, while his lonely partner waited.
    B. If you are well, will you come early?
    C. I think you have guessed right, though you were rather slow, I must say.
    D. The last hundred years have seen more change than a thousand years of the Roman Empire, than a hundred thousand years of the stone age.

Questions 18-24.

DIRECTIONS: Select the choice describing the error in the sentence.

18. If us seniors do not support school functions, who will? 18.____
    A. Unnecessary shift in tense B. Incomplete sentence
    C. Improper case of pronoun D. Lack of parallelism

19. The principal has issued regulations which, in my opinion, I think are too harsh. 19.____
    A. Incorrect punctuation B. Faulty sentence structure
    C. Misspelling D. Redundant expression

20. The freshmens' and sophomores' performances equaled those of the juniors and seniors. 20.____
    A. Ambiguous reference B. Incorrect placement of punctuation
    C. Misspelling of past tense D. Incomplete comparison

21. Each of them, Anne and her, is an outstanding pianist I can't tell you which one is best. 21.____
    A. Lack of agreement B. Improper degree of comparison
    C. Incorrect case of pronoun D. Run-on sentence

22. She wears clothes that are more expensive than my other friends. 22.____
    A. Misuse of *than* B. Incorrect relative pronoun
    C. Shift in tense D. Faulty comparison

23. At the very end of the story it implies that the children's father died tragically. 23.____
    A. Misuse of *implies* B. Indefinite use of pronoun
    C. Incorrect spelling D. Incorrect possessive

24. At the end of the game both of us, John and me, couldn't scarcely walk because we were so tired. 24.____
    A. Incorrect punctuation B. Run-on sentence
    C. Incorrect case of pronoun D. Double negative

Questions 25-30.

DIRECTIONS: Questions 25 through 30 consist of a sentence lacking certain needed punctuation. Pick as your answer the description of punctuation which will CORRECTLY complete the sentence.

25. If you take the time to keep up your daily correspondence you will no doubt be most efficient. 25.____
    A. Comma only after *doubt*
    B. Comma only after *correspondence*
    C. Commas after *correspondence*, *will*, and *be*
    D. Commas after *if*, *correspondence*, and *will*

26. Because he did not send the application soon enough he did not receive the up to date copy of the book.
    A. Commas after *application* and *enough, and quotation marks before* up *and after* date
    B. Commas after *application* and *enough,* and hyphens between *to* and *date*
    C. Comma after *enough,* and hyphens between *up* and *to* and between *to* and *date*
    D. Comma after *application,* and quotation marks before *up* and after *date*

27. The coordinator requested from the department the following items a letter each week summarizing progress personal forms and completed applications for tests.
    A. Commas after *items* and *completed*
    B. Semi-colon after *items* and *progress,* comma after *forms*
    C. Colon after *items,* commas after *progress* and *forms*
    D. Colon after *items,* commas after *forms* and *applications*

28. The supervisor asked Who will attend the conference next month.
    A. Comma after *asked,* period after *month*
    B. Period after *asked,* question mark after *month*
    C. Comma after *asked,* quotation marks before *Who,* quotation marks after *month,* and question mark after the quotation marks
    D. Comma after *asked,* quotation marks before *Who,* question mark after *month,* and quotation marks after the question mark

29. When the statistics are collected, we will forward the results to you as soon as possible.
    A. Comma after *you*
    B. Commas after *forward* and *you*
    C. Commas after *collected, results* and *you*
    D. Comma after *collected*

30. The ecology of our environment is concerned with mans pollution of the atmosphere.
    A. Comma after *ecology*
    B. Apostrophe after *n* and before *s* in *mans*
    C. Commas after *ecology* and *environment*
    D. Apostrophe after *s* in *mans*

KEY (CORRECT ANSWERS)

1.	D	11.	C	21.	B
2.	A	12.	D	22.	D
3.	D	13.	B	23.	B
4.	A	14.	A	24.	D
5.	B	15.	A	25.	B
6.	D	16.	A	26.	C
7.	A	17.	C	27.	C
8.	C	18.	C	28.	D
9.	A	19.	D	29.	D
10.	A	20.	B	30.	B

TEST 3

DIRECTIONS: Each question or incomplete statement is followed by several suggested answers or completions. Select the one that BEST answers the question or completes the statement. *PRINT THE LETTER OF THE CORRECT ANSWER IN THE SPACE AT THE RIGHT.*

Questions 1-6.

DIRECTIONS: From the four choices offered in Questions 1 through 6, select the one which is INCORRECT.

1. A. Before we try to extricate ourselves from this struggle in which we are now engaged in, we must be sure that we are not severing ties of honor and duty.
   B. Besides being an outstanding student, he is also a leader in school government and a trophy-winner in school sports.
   C. If the framers of the Constitution were to return to life for a day, their opinion of our amendments would be interesting.
   D. Since there are three m's in the word, it is frequently misspelled.

1.____

2. A. It was a college with an excellance beyond question.
   B. The coach will accompany the winners, whomever they may be.
   C. The dean, together with some other faculty members, is planning a conference.
   D. The jury are arguing among themselves.

2.____

3. A. This box is less nearly square than that one.
   B. Wagner is many persons' choice as the world's greatest composer.
   C. The habits of Copperheads are different from Diamond Backs.
   D. The teacher maintains that the child was insolent.

3.____

4. A. There was a time when the Far North was unknown territory. Now American soldiers manning radar stations there wave to Boeing jet planes zooming by overhead.
   B. Exodus, the psalms, and Deuteronomy are all books of the Old Testament.
   C. Linda identified her china dishes by marking their bottoms with india ink.
   D. Harry S. Truman, former president of the United States, served as a captain in the American army during World War I.

4.____

5. A. The sequel of their marriage was a divorce.
   B. We bought our car secondhand.
   C. His whereabouts is unknown.
   D. Jones offered to use his own car, providing the company would pay for gasoline, oil, and repairs,

5.____

6. A. I read Golding's "Lord of the Flies".
    B. The orator at the civil rights rally thrilled the audience when he said, "I quote Robert Burns's line, 'A man's a man for a' that."
    C. The phrase "producer to consumer" is commonly used by market analysts.
    D. The lawyer shouted, "Is not this evidence illegal?"

6.____

Questions 7-9.

DIRECTIONS: In answering Questions 7 through 9, mark the letter A if faulty because of incorrect grammar, mark the letter B if faulty because of incorrect punctuation, mark the letter C if correct.

7. Mr. Brown our accountant, will audit the accounts next week.

7.____

8. Give the assignment to whomever is able to do it most efficiently.

8.____

9. The supervisor expected either your or I to file these reports.

9.____

Questions 10-14.

DIRECTIONS: In each of the following groups of four sentences, one sentence contains an error in sentence structure, grammar, usage, diction, or punctuation. Indicate the INCORRECT sentence.

10. A. The agent asked, "Did you say, 'Never again?'"
    B. Kindly let me know whether you can visit us on the 17th.
    C. "I cannot accept that!" he exploded. "Please show me something else.
    D. Ed, will you please lend me your grass shears for an hour or so.

10.____

11. A. Recalcitrant though he may have been, Alexander was willfully destructive.
    B. Everybody should look out for himself.
    C. John is one of those students who usually spends most of his time in the principal's office.
    D. She seems to feel that what is theirs is hers.

11.____

12. A. Be he ever so much in the wrong, I'll support the man while deploring his actions.
    B. The schools' lack of interest in consumer education is shortsighted.
    C. I think that Fitzgerald's finest stanza is one which includes the reference to youth's "sweet-scented manuscript.
    D. I never would agree to Anderson having full control of the company's policies.

12.____

13. A. We had to walk about five miles before finding a gas station.
    B. The willful sending of a false alarm has, and may, result in homicide.
    C. Please bring that book to me at once.
    D. Neither my sister nor I am interested in bowling.

13.____

14. A. He is one of the very few football players who doesn't wear a helmet with a face guard.
    B. But three volunteers appeared at the recruiting office.
    C. Such consideration as you can give us will be appreciated.
    D. When I left them, the group were disagreeing about the proposed legislation.

14.____

Question 15.

DIRECTIONS: Question 15 contains two sentences concerning criminal law. The sentences could contain errors in English grammar or usage. A sentence does not contain an error simply because it could be written in a different manner. In answering this question, choose answer
A. if only sentence I is correct
B. if only sentence II is correct
C. if both sentences are correct
D. if neither sentence is correct

15. I. The use of fire or explosives to destroy tangible property is proscribed by the criminal mischief provisions of the Revised Penal Law.
    II. The defendant's taking of a taxicab for the immediate purpose of affecting his escape did not constitute grand larceny.

15.____

KEY (CORRECT ANSWERS)

1.	A	6.	A	11.	C
2.	B	7.	B	12.	D
3.	C	8.	A	13.	B
4.	B	9.	A	14.	A
5.	D	10	A	15.	A

SUPERVISION STUDY GUIDE

Social science has developed information about groups and leadership in general and supervisor-employee relationships in particular. Since organizational effectiveness is closely linked to the ability of supervisors to direct the activities of employees, these findings are important to executives everywhere.

IS A SUPERVISOR A LEADER?

First-line supervisors are found in all large business and government organizations. They are the men at the base of an organizational hierarchy. Decisions made by the head of the organization reach them through a network of intermediate positions. They are frequently referred to as part of the management team, but their duties seldom seem to support this description.

A supervisor of clerks, tax collectors, meat inspectors, or securities analysts is not charged with budget preparation. He cannot hire or fire the employees in his own unit on his say-so. He does not administer programs which require great planning, coordinating, or decision making.

Then what is he? He is the man who is directly in charge of a group of employees doing productive work for a business or government agency. If the work requires the use of machines, the men he supervises operate them. If the work requires the writing of reports, the men he supervises write them. He is expected to maintain a productive flow of work without creating problems which higher levels of management must solve. But is he a leader?

To carry out a specific part of an agency's mission, management creates a unit, staffs it with a group of employees and designates a supervisor to take charge of them. Management directs what this unit shall do, from time to time changes directions, and often indicates what the group should not do. Management presumably creates status for the supervisor by giving him more pay, a title, and special privileges.

Management asks a supervisor to get his workers to attain organizational goals, including the desired quantity and quality of production. Supposedly, he has authority to enable him to achieve this objective. Management at least assumes that by establishing the status of the supervisor's position, it has created sufficient authority to enable him to achieve these goals— not his goals, nor necessarily the group's, but management's goals.

In addition, supervision includes writing reports, keeping records of membership in a higher-level administrative group, industrial engineering, safety engineering, editorial duties, housekeeping duties, etc. The supervisor as a member of an organizational network, must be responsible to the changing demands of the management above him. At the same time, he must be responsive to the demands of the work group of which he is a member. He is placed in the difficult position of communicating and implementing new decisions, changed programs and revised production quotas for his work group, although he may have had little part in developing them.

It follows, then, that supervision has a special characteristic: achievement of goals, previously set by management, through the efforts of others. It is in this feature of the supervisor's job that we find the role of a leader in the sense of the following definition: *A leader is that person who <u>most</u> effectively influences group activities toward goal setting and goal achievements.*

This definition is broad. It covers both leaders in groups that come together voluntarily and in those brought together through a work assignment in a factory, store, or government agency. In the natural group, the authority necessary to attain goals is determined by the group membership and is granted by them. In the working group, it is apparent that the establishment of a supervisory position creates a predisposition on the part of employees to accept the authority of the occupant of that position. We cannot, however, assume that mere occupation confers authority sufficient to assure the accomplishment of an organization's goals.

Supervision is different, then, from leadership. The supervisor is expected to fulfill the role of leader but without obtaining a grant of authority from the group he supervises. The supervisor is expected to influence the group in the achieving of goals but is often handicapped by having little influence on the organizational process by which goals are set. The supervisor, because he works in an organizational setting, has the burdens of additional organizational duties and restrictions and requirements arising out of the fact that his position is subordinate to a hierarchy of higher-level supervisors. These differences between leadership and supervision are reflected in our definition: *Supervision is basically a leadership role, in a formal organization, which has as its objective the effective influencing of other employees.*

Even though these differences between supervision and leadership exist, a significant finding of experimenters in this field is that supervisors <u>must</u> be leaders to be successful.

The problem is: How can a supervisor exercise leadership in an organizational setting? We might say that the supervisor is expected to be a natural leader in a situation which does not come about naturally. His situation becomes really difficult in an organization which is more eager to make its supervisors into followers rather than leaders.

LEADERSHIP: NATURAL AND ORGANIZATIONAL

Leadership, in its usual sense of *natural* leadership, and supervision are not the same. In some cases, leadership embraces broader powers and functions than supervision; in other cases, supervision embraces more than leadership. This is true both because of the organization and technical aspects of the supervisor's job and because of the relatively freer setting and inherent authority of the natural leader.

The natural leader usually has much more authority and influence than the supervisor. Group members not only follow his command but prefer it that way. The employee, however, can appeal the supervisor's commands to his union or to the supervisor's superior or to the personnel office. These intercessors represent restrictions on the supervisor's power to lead.

The natural leader can gain greater membership involvement in the group's objectives, and he can change the objectives of the group. The supervisor can attempt to gain employee support only for management's objectives; he cannot set other objectives. In these instances leadership is broader than supervision.

The natural leader must depend upon whatever skills are available when seeking to attain objectives. The supervisor is trained in the administrative skills necessary to achieve management's goals. If he does not possess the requisite skills, however, he can call upon management's technicians.

A natural leader can maintain his leadership, in certain groups, merely by satisfying members' need for group affiliation. The supervisor must maintain his leadership by directing and organizing his group to achieve specific organizational goals set for him and his group by management. He must have a technical competence and a kind of coordinating ability which is not needed by many natural leaders.

A natural leader is responsible only to his group which grants him authority. The supervisor is responsible to management, which employs him, and also to the work group of which he is a member. The supervisor has the exceedingly difficult job of reconciling the demands of two groups frequently in conflict. He is often placed in the untenable position of trying to play two antagonistic roles. In the above instance, supervision is broader than leadership.

ORGANIZATIONAL INFLUENCES ON LEADERSHIP

The supervisor is both a product and a prisoner of the organization wherein we find him. The organization which creates the supervisor's position also obstructs, restricts, and channelizes the exercise of his duties. These influences extend beyond prescribed functional relationships to specific supervisory behavior. For example, even in a face-to-face situation involving one of his subordinates, the supervisor's actions are controlled to a great extent by his organization. His behavior must conform to the organization policy on human relations, rules which dictate personnel procedures, specific prohibitions governing conduct, the attitudes of his own superior, etc. He is not a free agent operating within the limits of his work group. His freedom of action is much more circumscribed than is generally admitted. The organizational influences which limit his leadership actions can be classified as structure, prescriptions, and proscriptions.

The organizational structure places each supervisor's position in context with other designated positions. It determines the relationships between his position and specific positions which impinge on his. The structure of the organization designates a certain position to which he looks for orders and information about his work. It gives a particular status to his position within a pattern of statuses from which he perceives that (1) certain positions are on a par, organizationally, with his, (2) other positions are subordinate, and (3) still others are superior.

The organizational structure determines those positions to which he should look for advice and assistance, and those positions to which he should give advice and assistance.

For instance, the organizational structure has predetermined that the supervisor of a clerical processing unit shall report to a supervisory position in a higher echelon. He shall have certain relationships with the supervisors of the work units which transmit work to and receive work from his unit. He shall discuss changes and clarification of procedures with certain staff units, such as organization and methods, cost accounting, and personnel. He shall consult supervisors of units which provide or receive special work assignments.

The organizational structure, however, establishes patterns other than those of the relationships of positions. These are the patterns of responsibility, authority, and expectations.

The supervisor is responsible for certain activities or results; he is presumably invested with the authority to achieve these. His set of authority and responsibility is interwoven with other sets to the end that all goals and functions of the organization are parceled out in small, manageable lots. This, of course, establishes a series of expectations: a single supervisor can perform his particular set of duties only upon the assumption that preceding or contiguous sets of duties have been, or are being carried out. At the same time, he is aware of the expectations of others that he will fulfill his functional role.

The structure of an organization establishes relationships between specified positions and specific expectations for these positions. The fact that these relationships and expectations are established is one thing; whether or not they are met is another.

PRESCRIPTIONS AND PROSCRIPTIONS

But let us return to the organizational influences which act to restrict the supervisor's exercise of leadership. These are the prescriptions and proscriptions generally in effect in all organizations, and those peculiar to a single organization. In brief these are the *thou shalt's* and the *thou shalt not's*.

Organizations not only prescribe certain duties for individual supervisory positions, they also prescribe specific methods and means of carrying out these duties and maintaining management-employee relations. These include rules, regulations, policy, and tradition. It does no good for the supervisor to say, *This seems to be the best way to handle such-and-such,* if the organization has established a routine for dealing with problems. For good or bad, there are rules that state that firings shall be executed in such a manner, accompanied by a certain notification; that training shall be conducted, and in this manner. Proscriptions are merely negative prescriptions; you may not discriminate against any employee because of politics or race; you shall not suspend any employee without following certain procedures and obtaining certain approvals.

Most of these prohibitions and rules apply to the area of interpersonal relations, precisely the area which is now arousing most interest on the part of administrators and managers. We have become concerned about the contrast between formally prescribed relationships and interpersonal relationships, and this brings us to the often discussed informal organization.

FORMAL AND INFORMAL ORGANIZATIONS

As we well know, the functions and activities of any organization are broken down into individual units of work called positions. Administrators must establish a pattern which will link these positions to each other and relate them to a system of authority and responsibility. Man-to-man are spelled out as plainly as possible for all to understand. Managers, then, build an official structure which we call the formal organization.

In these same organizations, employees react individually and in groups to institutionally determined roles. John, a worker, rides in the same carpool as Joe, a foreman. An unplanned communication develops. Harry, a machinist knows more about high-speed machining than his foreman or anyone else in his shop. An unofficial tool boss comes into being. Mary, who fought with Jane, is promoted over her. Jane now gives Mary's directions. A planned relationship fails to develop. The employees have built a structure which we call the informal organization.

Formal organization is a system of management-prescribed relations between positions in an organization.

Informal organization is a network of unofficial relations between people in an organization.

These definitions might lead us to the absurd conclusion that positions carry out formal activities and that employe4es spend their time in unofficial activities. We must recognize that organizational activities are in all cases carried out by people. The formal structure provides a needed framework within which interpersonal relations occur. What we call informal organization is the complex of normal, natural relations among employees. These personal relationships may be negative or positive. That is, they may impede or aid the achievement of organizational goals. For example, friendship between two supervisors greatly increases the probability of good cooperation and coordination between their sections. On the other hand, *buck passing* nullifies the formal structure by failure to meet a prescribed and expected responsibility.

It is improbable that an ideal organization exists where all activities are carried out in strict conformity to a formally prescribed pattern of functional roles. Informal organization arises because of the incompleteness and ambiguities in the network of formally prescribed relationships, or in response to the needs or inadequacies of supervisors or managers who hold prescribed functional roles in an organization. Many of these relationships are not prescribed by the organizational pattern; many cannot be prescribed; many should not be prescribed.

Management faces the problem of keeping the informal organization in harmony with the mission of the agency. One way to do this is to make sure that all employees have a clear understanding of and are sympathetic with that mission. The issuance of organizational charts, procedural manuals, and functional descriptions of the work to be done by divisions and sections helps communicate management's plans and goals. Issuances alone, of course, cannot do the whole job. They should be accompanied by oral discussion and explanation. Management must ensure that there is mutual understanding and acceptance of charts and procedures. More important is that management acquaint itself with the attitudes, activities, and peculiar brands of logic which govern the informal organization. Only through this type of knowledge can they and supervisors keep informal goals consistent with the agency mission.

SUPERVISION STATUS AND FUNCTIONAL ROLE

A well-established supervisor is respected by the employees who work with him. They defer to his wishes. It is clear that a superior-subordinate relationship has been established. That is, status of the supervisor has been established in relation to other employees of the same work group. This same supervisor gains the respect of employees when he behaves in as certain manner. He will be expected, generally, to follow the customs of the group in such matters as dress, recreation, and manner of speaking. The group has a set of expectations as to his behavior. His position is a functional role which carries with it a collection of rights and obligations.

The position of supervisor usually has a status distinct from the individual who occupies it: it is much like a position description which exists whether or not there is an incumbent. The status of a supervisory position is valued higher than that of an employee position both because of the functional role of leadership which is assigned to it and because of the status symbols of titles, rights, and privileges which go with it.

Social ranking, or status, is not simple because it involves both the position and the man. An individual may be ranked higher than others because of his education, social background, perceived leadership ability, or conformity to group customs and ideals. If such a man is ranked higher by the members of a work group than their supervisor, the supervisor's effectiveness may be seriously undermined.

If the organization does not build and reinforce a supervisor's status, his position can be undermined in a different way. This will happen when managers go around rather than through the supervisor or designate him as a straw boss, acting boss, or otherwise not a real boss.

Let us clarify this last point. A role, and corresponding status, establishes a set of expectations. Employees expect their supervisor to do certain things and to act in certain ways. They are prepared to respond to that expected behavior. When the supervisor's behavior does not conform to their expectations, they are surprised, confused, and ill-at-ease. It becomes necessary for them to resolve their confusion, if they can. They might do this by turning to one of their own members for leadership. If the confusion continues, or their attempted solutions are not satisfactory, they will probably become a poorly motivated, non-cohesive group which cannot function very well.

COMMUNICATION AND THE SUPERVISOR

In a recent survey, railroad workers reported that they rarely look to their supervisor for information about the company. This is startling, at least to us, because we ordinarily think of the supervisor as the link between management and worker. We expect the supervisor to be the prime source of information about the company. Actually, the railroad workers listed the supervisor next to last in the o5rder of their sources of information. Most surprising of all, the supervisors, themselves, stated that rumor and unofficial contacts were their principal sources of information. Here we see one of the reasons why supervisors may not be as effective as management desires.

The supervisor is not only being bypassed by his work group, he is being ignored, and his position weakened, by the very organization which is holding him responsible for the activities of his workers. If he is management's representative to the employee, then management has an obligation to keep him informed of its activities. This is necessary if he is to carry out his functions efficiently and maintain his leadership in the work group. The supervisor is expected to be a source of information; when he is not, his status is not clear, and employees are dissatisfied because he has not lived up to expectations.

By providing information to the supervisor to pass along to employees, we can strengthen his position as leader of the group, and increase satisfaction and cohesion within the group. Because he has more information than the other members, receives information sooner, and passes it along at the proper times, members turn to him as a source and also provide him with information in the hope of receiving some in return. From this, we can see an increase in group cohesiveness because:

- Employees are bound closer to their supervisor because he is *in the know*.
- There is less need to go outside the group for answers
- Employees will more quickly turn to the supervisor for enlightenment

The fact that he has the answers will also enhance the supervisor's standing in the eyes of his men. This increased status will serve to bolster his authority and control of the group and will probably result in improved morale and productivity.

The foregoing, of course, does not mean that all management information should be given out. There are obviously certain policy determinations and discussions which need not or cannot be transmitted to all supervisors. However, the supervisor must be kept as fully informed as possible so that he can answer questions when asked and can allay needless fears and anxieties. Further, the supervisor has the responsibility of encouraging employee questions and submissions of information. He must be able to present information to employees so that it is clearly understood and accepted. His attitude and manner should make it clear that he believes in what he is saying, that the information is necessary or desirable to the group, and that he is prepared to act on the basis of the information.

SUPERVISION AND JOB PERFORMANCE

The productivity of work groups is a product; employees' efforts are multiplied by the supervision they receive. Many investigators have analyzed this relationship and have discovered elements of supervision which differentiate high and low production groups. These researchers have identified certain types of supervisory practices which they classify as *employee-centered* and other types which they classify as *production centered*.

The difference between these two kinds of supervision lies not in specific practices but in the approach or orientation to supervision. The employee-centered supervisor directs most of his efforts toward increasing employee motivation. He is concerned more with realizing the potential energy of persons than with administrative and technological methods of increasing efficiency and productivity. He is the man who finds ways of causing employees to want to work harder with the same tools. These supervisors emphasize the personal relations between their employees and themselves.

Now, obviously, these pictures are overdrawn. No one supervisor has all the virtues of the ideal type of employee-centered supervisor. And, fortunately, no one supervisor has all the bad traits found in many production-centered supervisors. We should remember that the various practices that researchers have fond which distinguish these two kinds of supervision represent the many practices and methods of supervisors of all gradations between these extremes. We should be careful, too, of the implications of the labels attached to the two types. For instance, being production-centered is not necessarily bad, since the principal responsibility of any supervisor is maintaining the production level that is expected of his work group. Being employee-centered may not necessarily be good, if the only result is a happy, chuckling crew of loafers. To return to the researchers' findings, employee-centered supervisors:

- Recommend promotions, transfers, pay increases
- Inform men about what is happening in the company
- Keep men posted on how well they are doing
- Hear complaints and grievances sympathetically
- Speak up for subordinates

Production-centered supervisors, on the other hand, don't do those things. They check on employees more frequently, give more detailed and frequent instructions, don't give reasons for changes, and are more punitive when mistakes are made. Employee-centered supervisors were reported to contribute to high morale and high production, whereas production-centered supervision was associated with lower morale and less production.

More recent findings, however, show that the relationship between supervision and productivity is not this simple. Investigators now report that high production is more frequently associated with supervisory practices which combine employee-centered behavior with concern for production. (This concern is not the same, however, as anxiety about production, which is the hallmark of our production-centered supervisor.) Let us examine these apparently contradictory findings and the premises from which they are derived.

SUPERVISION AND MORALE

Why do supervisory activities cause high or low production? As the name implies, the activities of the employee-centered supervisor tend to relate him more closely and satisfactorily to his workers. The production-centered supervisor's practices tend to separate him from his group and to foster antagonism. An analysis of this difference may answer our question.

Earlier, we pointed out that the supervisor is a type of leader and that leadership is intimately related to the group in which it occurs We discover, now, that an employee-centered supervisor's primary activities are concerned with both his leadership and his group membership. Such a supervisor is a member of a group and occupies a leadership role in that group.

These facts are sometimes obscured when we speak of the supervisor as management's representative, or as the organizational link between management and the employee, or as the end of the chain of command. If we really want to understand what it is we expect of the supervisor, we must remember that he is the designated leader of a group of employees to whom he is bound by interaction and interdependence.

Most of his actions are aimed, consciously or unconsciously, at strengthening membership ties in the group. This includes both making members more conscious that he is a member of their group) and causing members to identify themselves more closely with the group. These ends are accomplished by:

- making the group more attractive to the worker: they find satisfaction of their needs for recognition, friendship, enjoyable work, etc.;
- maintaining open communication: employees can express their views and obtain information about the organization
- giving assistance: members can seek advice on personal problems as well as their work; and
- acting as a buffer between the group and management: he speaks up for his men and explains the reasons for management's decisions.

Such actions both strengthen group cohesiveness and solidarity and affirm the supervisor's leadership position in the group.

DEFINING MORALE

This brings us back to a point mentioned earlier. We had said that employee-centered supervisors contribute to high morale as well as to high production. But how can we explain units which have low morale and high productivity, or vice versa? Usually production and morale are considered separately, partly because they are measured against different criteria and partly because, in some instances, they seem to be independent of each other.

Some of this difficulty may stem from confusion over definitions of morale. Morale has been defined as, or measured by, absences from work, satisfaction with job or company, dissension among members of work groups, productivity, apathy or lack of interest, readiness to help others, and a general aura of happiness as rated by observers. Some of these criteria of morale are not subject to the influence of the supervisor, and some of them are not clearly related to productivity. Definitions like these invite findings of low morale coupled with high production.

Both productivity and morale can be influenced by environmental factors not under the control of group members or supervisors. Such things as plant layout, organizational structure and goals, lighting, ventilation, communications, and management planning may have an adverse or desirable effect.

We might resolve the dilemma by defining morale on the basis of our understanding of the supervisor as leader of a group; morale is the degree of satisfaction of group members with their leadership. In this light, the supervisor's employee-centered activities bear a clear relation to morale. His efforts to increase employee identification with the group and to strengthen his leadership lead to greater satisfaction with that leadership. By increasing group cohesiveness and by demonstrating that his influence and power can aid the group, he is able to enhance his leadership status and afford satisfaction to the group.

SUPERVISION, PRODUCTION, AND MORALE

There are factors within the organization itself which determine whether increased production is possible:

- Are production goals expressed in terms understandable to employees and are they realistic?
- Do supervisors responsible for production respect the agency mission and production goals?
- If employees do not know how to do the job well, does management provide a trainer—often the supervisor—who can teach efficient work methods?

There are other factors within the work group which determine whether increased production will be attained:

- Is leadership present which can bring about the desired level of production?
- Are production goals accepted by employees as reasonable and attainable?
- If group effort is involved, are members able to coordinate their efforts?

Research findings confirm the view that an employee-centered supervisor can achieve higher morale than a production-centered supervisor. Managers may well ask what is the relationship between this and production.

Supervision is production-oriented to the extent that it focuses attention on achieving organizational goals, and plans and devises methods for attaining them; it is employee-centered to the extent that it focuses attention on employee attitudes toward those goals, and plans and works toward maintenance of employee satisfaction.

High productivity and low morale result when a supervisor plans and organizes work efficiently but cannot achieve high membership satisfaction. Low production and high morale result when a supervisor, though keeping members satisfied with his leadership, either has not gained acceptance of organizational goals or does not have the technical competence to achieve them.

The relationship between supervision, morale, and productivity is an interdependent one, with the supervisor playing an integral role due to his ability to influence productivity and morale independently of each other.

A supervisor who can plan his work well has good technical knowledge, and who can install better production methods can raise production without necessarily increasing group satisfaction. On the other hand, a supervisor who can motivate his employees and keep them satisfied with his leadership can gain high production in spite of technical difficulties and environmental obstacles.

CLIMATE AND SUPERVISION

Climate, the intangible environment of an organization made up of attitudes, beliefs, and traditions, plays a large part in morale, productivity, and supervision. Usually when we speak of climate and its relationship to morale and productivity, we talk about the merits of *democratic* versus *authoritarian* climate. Employees seem to produce more and have higher morale in a democratic climate, whereas in an authoritarian climate, the reverse seems to be true or so the researchers tell us. We would do well to determine what these terms mean to supervision.

Perhaps most of our difficulty in understanding and applying these concepts comes from our emotional reactions to the words themselves. For example, authoritarian climate is usually painted as the very blackest kind of dictatorship. This is not surprising, because we are usually expected to believe that it is invariably bad. Conversely, democratic climate is drawn to make the driven snow look impure by comparison.

Now these descriptions are most probably true when we talk about our political processes, or town meetings, or freedom of speech. However, the same labels have been used by social scientists in other contexts and have also been applied to government and business organizations, without it, it seems, any recognition that the meanings and their social values may have changed somewhat

For example, these labels were used in experiments conducted in an informal classroom setting using 11-year-old boys as subjects. The descriptive labels applied to the climate of the setting as well as the type of leadership practiced. When these labels were transferred to a management setting, it seems that many presumed that they principally meant the king of leadership rather than climate. We can see that there is a great difference between the experimental and management settings and that leadership practices for one might be inappropriate for the other.

It is doubtful that formal work organizations can be anything but authoritarian, in that goals are set by management and a hierarchy exists through which decisions and orders from the top are transmitted downward. Organizations are authoritarian by structure and need; direction and control are placed in the hands of a few in order to gain fast and efficient decision making. Now this does not mean to describe a dictatorship. It is merely the recognition of the fact that direction of organizational affairs comes from above. It should be noted that leadership in some natural groups is, in this sense, authoritarian.

Granting that formal organizations have this kind of authoritarian leadership, can there be a democratic climate? Certainly there can be, but we would want to define and delimit this term. A more realistic meaning of democratic climate in organizations is the use of permissive and participatory methods in management-employee relations. That is, a mutual exchange of information and explanation with the granting of individual freedom within certain restricted and defined limits. However, it is not our purpose to debate the merits of authoritarianism versus democracy. We recognize that within the small work group there is a need for freedom from constraint and an increase in participation in order to achieve organizational goals within the framework of the organizational movement.

Another aspect of climate is best expressed by this familiar, and true, saying: actions speak louder than words. Of particular concern to us is this effect of management climate on the behavior of supervisors, particularly in employee-centered activities.

There have been reports of disappointment with efforts to make supervisors ore employee-centered. Managers state that, since research has shown ways of improving human relations, supervisors should begin to practice these methods. Usually a training course in human relations is established; and supervisors are given this training. Managers then sit back and wait for the expected improvements, only to find that there are none.

If we wish to produce changes in the supervisor's behavior, the climate must be made appropriate and rewarding to the changed behavior. This means that top-level attitudes and behavior cannot deny or contradict the change we are attempting to effect. Basic changes in organizational behavior cannot be made with any permanence, unless we provide an environment that is receptive to the changes and rewards those persons who do change.

IMPROVING SUPERVISION

Anyone who has read this far might expect to find *A Dozen Rules for Dealing With Employees* or *29 Steps to Supervisory Success*. We will not provide such a list.

Simple rules suffer from their simplicity. They ignore the complexities of human behavior. Reliance upon rules may cause supervisors to concentrate on superficial aspects of their relations with employees. It may preclude genuine understanding.

The supervisor who relies on a list of rules tends to think of people in mechanistic terms. In a certain situation, he uses *Rule No. 3*. Employees are not treated as thinking and feeling persons, but rather as figures in a formula: Rule 3 applied to employee X = Production.

Employees usually recognize mechanical manipulation and become dissatisfied and resentful. They lose faith in, and respect for, their supervisor, and this may be reflected in lower morale and productivity.

We do not mean that supervisors must become social science experts if they wish to improve. Reports of current research indicate that there are two major parts of their job which can be strengthened through self-improvement: (1) Work planning, including technical skills, and (2) motivation of employees.

The most effective supervisors combine excellence in the administrative and technical aspects of their work with friendly and considerate personal relations with their employees.

CRITICAL PERSONAL RELATIONS

Later in this chapter we shall talk about administrative aspects of supervision, but first let us comment on *friendly and considerate personal relations*. We have discussed this subject throughout the preceding chapters, but we want to review some of the critical supervisory influences on personal relations.

Closeness of Supervision: The closeness of supervision has an important effect on productivity and morale. Mann and Dent found that supervisors of low-producing units supervise very closely, while high-producing supervisors exercise only general supervision. It was found that the low-producing supervisors:

- check on employees more frequently
- give more detailed and frequent instructions
- limit employee's freedom to do job in own way

Workers who felt less closely supervised reported that they were better satisfied with their jobs and the company. We should note that the manner or attitude of the supervisor has an important bearing on whether employees perceive supervision as being close or general.

These findings are another way of saying that supervision does not mean standing over the employee and telling him what to do and when and how to do it. The more effective supervisor tells his employees what is required, giving general instructions.

COMMUNICATION

Supervisors of high-production units consider communication as one of the most important aspects of their job. Effective communication is used by these supervisors to achieve better interpersonal relations and improved employee motivation. Low-production supervisors do not rate communications as highly important.

High-producing supervisors find that an important aid to more effective communication is listening. They are ready to listen to both personal problems or interests and questions about the work. This does not mean that they are *nosey* or meddle in their employees' personal lives, but rather that they show a willingness to listen, and do listen, if their employees wish to discuss problems.

These supervisors inform employees about forthcoming changes in work; they discuss agency policy with employees; and they make sure that each employee knows how well he is doing. What these supervisors do is use two-way communication effectively. Unless the supervisor freely imparts information, he will not receive information in return.

Attitudes and perception are frequently affected by communication or the lack of it. Research surveys reveal that many supervisors are not aware of their employees' attitudes, nor do they know what personal reactions their supervision arouses. Through frank discussion with employees, they have been surprised to discover employee beliefs about which they were ignorant. Discussion sometimes reveals that the supervisor and his employees have totally different impressions about the same event. The supervisor should be constantly on the alert for misconceptions about his words and deeds. He must remember that, although his actions are perfectly clear to himself, they may be, and frequently are, viewed differently by employees.

Failure to communicate information results in misconceptions and false assumptions. What you say and how you say it will strongly affect your employees' attitudes and perceptions. By giving them available information, you can prevent misconceptions; by discussion, you may be able to change attitudes; by questioning, you can discover what the perceptions and assumptions really are. And it need hardly be added that actions should conform very closely to words.

If we were to attempt to reduce the above discussion on communication to rules, we would have a long list which would be based on one cardinal principle: Don't make assumptions!

- Don't assume that your employees know; tell them.
- Don't assume that you know how they feel; find out.
- Don't assume that they understand; clarify.

20 SUPERVISORY HINTS

1. Avoid inconsistency.
2. Always give employees a chance to explain their action before taking disciplinary action. Don't allow too much time for a "cooling off" period before disciplining an employee.
3. Be specific in your criticisms.
4. Delegate responsibility wisely.
5. Do not argue or lose your temper, and avoid being impatient.
6. Promote mutual respect and be fair, impartial, and open-minded.
7. Keep in mind that asking for employees' advice and input can be helpful in decision making.
8. If you make promises, keep them.
9. Always keep the feelings, abilities, dignity and motives of your staff in mind.
10. Remain loyal to your employees' interests.
11. Never criticize employees in front of others, or treat employees like children.
12. Admit mistakes. Don't place blame on your employees, or make excuses.
13. Be reasonable in your expectations, give complete instructions, and establish well-planned goals.
14. Be knowledgeable about office details and procedures, but avoid becoming bogged down in details.
15. Avoid supervising too closely or too loosely. Employees should also view you as an approachable supervisor.
16. Remember that employees' personal problems may affect job performance, but become involved only when appropriate.
17. Work to develop workers, and to instill a feeling of cooperation while working toward mutual goals.
18. Do not overpraise or underpraise, be properly appreciative.
19. Never ask an employee to discipline someone for you.
20. A complaint, even if unjustified, should be taken seriously.

NOTES

CHILD DEVELOPMENT

I - MIDDLE YEARS: AGES 6-12

The ages six to twelve are commonly known as the middle years of childhood. This is the time when children are in full bloom: they are no longer babies but the demands of adult life are still far away. All through this period children continue to develop their special personalities. They are getting to know more about themselves and the world in which they live, and their slow, steady growth can be observed. They grow in independence and are more able to take care of themselves. They also are eager adventurers who learn from their explorations but who often find, to their dismay and to the dismay of the adults around them, that they still have a lot to learn.

Each child is different and there are no set rules for rearing or teaching children. How children grow depends on the characteristics they inherit from their parents and, to a great extent, it depends on the guidance provided by parents and other adults. It also depends on the experiences they have inside and outside of their homes.

Although each child's temperament makes her special, certain guidelines of child growth apply to most youngsters, and parents and other caregivers may find these guidelines helpful when working with the middle-years child.

Physical Development

Growth is of many different kinds and a child's development during the middle years includes increases in height, weight, and strength. The different rates of growth of various body parts account for the awkwardness of the youngster in the late childhood years. Height and weight increase much more slowly and evenly during the middle years than in early childhood. Children usually gain about two or three inches in height each year. Just as height increases at a slow steady pace, so, too, does weight. At the age of six, a child will be about seven times his birth weight. For example, a child who weighed seven pounds at birth will weigh almost fifty pounds at age six. Body proportions also change. The trunk becomes slimmer and more elongated in contrast to the chunky body of the preschooler. The chest becomes broader and flatter, causing the shoulders to droop. Arms and legs become long and thin with little evidence of muscles. It is this thinning-out of the trunk, combined with the elongation of the arms and legs, that gives the middle-years child the "all arms and legs" gawky appearance.

Sexual Differentiation

During the middle years, boys and girls gradually become aware of sexual differences in behavior, attitudes, and manners. These sex differences still can be seen in many play activities. Fortunately, however, both boys and girls now receive more encouragement to try activities traditionally reserved for the opposite sex. This helps to break down sex-role stereotypes. For example, girls learn that they can be good at tasks requiring physical skill, and boys learn that they can be caring young persons without losing their "masculinity." Opportunities for different kinds of play also mean that children develop a variety of skills to carry with them into adulthood.

Psychological Development

Middle-years children can find themselves in conflict with the need to grow up and the desire to remain a child forever, a conflict known as the Peter Pan fantasy. They want to grow up so that they can enjoy the prerogatives of adult life: staying up late, driving the car, wearing adult-styled clothes, and being privy to adult secrets. They want to be able to understand and laugh at adult jokes and be accepted into adult confidences and discussions.

On the other hand, they also want to hold on to all the privileges of childhood. Boys who quarrel, fight, and roughhouse and girls who dress up in their mothers' clothing and makeup are regarded as amusing by adults who would not tolerate such behavior in teenagers.

Social Development

There is a culture of childhood that is passed on solely by oral tradition. Many childrens' games, like hopscotch, marbles, kick-the-can, and blindman's buff, are passed down verbally from one generation to the next. Jokes, riddles, and sayings also are transmitted orally.

Georgie Porgie, pudding and pie Kissed the girls and made them cry.
or
Sticks and stones may break my bones, But names will never hurt me.
or
Ladybug, ladybug fly away home. Your house is on fire your children are gone Except for the little one under the stone Ladybug, ladybug fly away home.
or
Rain, rain go away
Come again another day.

This culture of childhood that finds itself rooted in the past gives a clue to the child's relationship to her family. In contrast to the upheaval an adolescent experiences, the young child may appear to be a staid traditionalist who accepts the authority of the family just as she accepts the games and superstitions of previous generations of children. The middle-years child is more likely to defend than attack her family and what it stands for. The family is the main base of security and identity and is still more important than the child's peer group.

Ages and Stages

Information presented here about the ages and stages of children is only a *guide* for adults working with children. Physically, emotionally, and intellectually, each child grows and develops at his own rate. Some youngsters may be early bloomers. That is, they may have reached a stage of emotional or physical development beyond their chronological years. It is not unusual for a six-year-old to be as tall as a ten-year-old. But when interacting with this child, adults must remember that he *is* six and not ten and they should not expect him to behave as though he were a ten-year-old. Another example is an eight-year-old with an extensive vocabulary who can converse with adults as though she were twelve. In a relationship with this child, it is important for adults to remember that although she may be conversationally mature, she may be mentally, physically and emotionally still an eight-year-old.

Understanding the characteristics of an age can be helpful to adults who work with or care for children. But, if adults are to foster optimal growth and development in children, they also must remain sensitive and responsive to children as individuals.

Six-Year-Olds

General
The sixth year is the age of transition.
• At this age, children are active, outgoing, and self-centered. Their own activities take precedence over everything else.
• They are in constant motion: jiggling, shoving, and pushing. They like to roughhouse and their play may go too far because they don't know when to stop.
• They can play organized games with rules, but only at beginning levels because strategy and foresight are not highly developed at the age of six.
• Six-year-olds may be clumsy and tend to dawdle. For example, they may be slow at dressing to go to school or other places. On the other hand, they want their needs met at once and get upset when adults do not drop everything to do their bidding.

Self-Concept and Independence
• They want to be the center of everything to be first and to win. They are the center of their very own universe and their way of

doing things seems the best and only way. They do not lose gracefully or accept criticism.

• They are assertive, bossy, and extremely sensitive to real or imagined slights. They dominate every situation and are always ready with advice.

• Growing up may be a strain at times for six-year-olds and there may be a period of regression during which they engage in baby talk and display babyish behavior.

• Six-year-olds are extremely possessive of their belongings.

• When the outside world impinges adversely upon them, they are stubborn, obstinate, and unreasonable.

• They tend to project their own feelings onto others and then criticize other people because of this. "She thinks she's-everything" or "He's so fresh."

• They are ashamed of their mistakes and fears and of being seen crying and are careful not to expose themselves to criticism.

Relating to Other Children and Adults

• Six-year-olds often pair up and have best friends with whom they spend a good deal of time. Such pairs often take pleasure in "keeping out" a third child who wants to join them.

• Friendships are erratic and may change many times. Lots of tattling and putting-down of other children goes on, for example, "He's dumb."

• Boys and girls occasionally play together at this age, but the movement toward same-sexed friends has already begun.

• Six-year-olds can be highly sensitive to their parents' moods. For instance, they are quick to notice changes in facial expressions.

Although the six-year-old is most loving of his mother, he is also building his sense of self by trying to break away from her. Many temper tantrums are directed at her and the six-year-old may often refuse to obey his mother's directions. On the other hand, the six-year-old can be sympathetic toward his mother when she is not feeling well.

Parents can find the six-year-old trying. Adults working with six-year-olds need to keep a sense of perspective and their sense of humor. If parents and other caregivers remember the transitional nature of this age, six will become a more manageable and less trying age.

Games and Activities

• Their activities center on the physical. Riding a bicycle is an activity they enjoy. Roller skating and swimming also are favorites.

• They are poor at games requiring strategy and foresight like chess, checkers, and tic-tac-toe, but like running games such as tag and hide-and-seek.

• Six-year-olds like making things as well as cooking activities. They also like to paint, color, and draw.

Seven-Year-Olds

General

Seven is the age of quieting down.

• Toward the beginning of the seventh year the child begins to assimilate the wealth of new experiences and information she learned in first grade.

• They begin to sift and sort information into categories and link the bits of information that they have acquired. Seven-year-olds begin to reason and may at times appear serious and reflective.

• Seven-year-olds can be moody and brooding and pensive and sad because their assimilation of knowledge is not always smooth. Action has shifted and may now take place within their minds rather than within a physical space.

• Although they are self-absorbed they are not isolationists. They are becoming more aware not only of themselves, but of others as well.

Self-Concept and Independence

- The increased introspection of seven-year-olds also means that they have an increased sense of self and are acquiring sensitivity to the reactions of others. This sensitivity is to what others do and say, but not to what other people think. To the seven-year-old, thinking and doing are the same thing.
- They are sensitive about their bodies, which they do not like to have exposed or touched, and they may refuse to use the bathroom at school if it has no door on it.
- Because the physical self and the psychic self are so closely related at this stage, seven-year-olds are reluctant to expose themselves to failure and criticism. They often leave the scene rather than put themselves in a position where they might be subject to criticism or disapproval.

Relating to Other Children and Adults

- They want to be helpful and to become real members of the family group.
- They can take on tasks and responsibilities. When performing chores, they are careful and persistent, and they will demand guidance from adults as to "What do we do now?" or "How do we do this?"
- They can be polite and considerate toward adults. Seven-year-olds are less resistant and less stubborn than six-year-olds.
- They play easily with other children and seem to be in control. Although they are active and boisterous, they know when to stop before someone gets hurt.

Games and Activities

- Seven-year-olds have more capacity to play alone than they had at six, and they enjoy solitary activities such as reading and drawing.
- Group play is still not well organized and is carried out to individual ends.
- They like building things but need to know where things go and where they end. They can understand a simple model and a blueprint.
- Seven-year-olds continue to skate, swim, and are better at bike riding.
- They are avid collectors of anything and everything from stones to bottle tops.
- Seven-year-olds are fond of table games and jigsaw puzzles and can tackle a complicated game like Monopoly.

Eight-Year-Olds
General

Eight-year-olds are expansive, but on a higher level than when they were six.

- They are outgoing, curious, and extremely social and self-confident.
- They tend to be critical of themselves and judgmental of others.
- They now concern themselves with the why of events, and they are active and expansive as they seek out new experiences.
- Eight-year-olds talk constantly and love to gossip.

Self-Concept and Independence

- Eight-year-olds have a greater awareness of self; they are less sensitive, less introspective, and less apt to withdraw. They are becoming individuals who are aware of themselves in the social world.
- They are able to judge and appraise themselves and are conscious of the ways in which they differ from other people.
- Eight-year-olds are concerned about how other people feel about them, and they can be demanding in their efforts to get information about themselves.
- They can work independently, but need direction.

Relating to Other Children and Adults

- Eight-year-olds are mature in their social relationships with others. Relationships with friends are positive. Friendships are closer and very important.
- There is a noticeable separation between boys and girls and both play at games that tend to exclude the opposite sex.

- They are usually friendly and cooperative, preferring mature jobs that resemble adult-like activities.
- They are more polite with strangers than they are at home and are able to hold their own in conversations with adults.

Games and Activities

- Eight-year-olds dislike playing alone. They prefer to be with an adult or another child. Action becomes the focus of all their play.
- Both boys and girls like cooking and baking and show an interest in foreign places and children from different times.
- The collections they began at seven now become more organized and classified.
- They tend to make up their own rules for games and they may even invent new games.
- Eight-year-olds like dramatic play, especially where they take the role of characters they have read about, seen, or heard about.
- Table games such as cards, parchesi, checkers, and dominoes are very popular.

When working with eight-year-olds, adults must remember that they are very social and like to be with peers. They gossip and talk constantly, passing notes from one to the other. This often gets out-of-hand when they are in group situations. In addition to their tendency to judge others, eight-year-olds are increasingly self-critical. For example, many children who liked artwork at six or seven may give it up at eight because they see the difference between the quality of their drawings and those of a friend.

In Summary

Children are individuals with their own special temperaments and idiosyncracies. The ages and stages children go through can vary tremendously from one child to the next and, by respecting the variousness of children, parents and other caregivers can help them develop strong and healthy self-concepts.

II - MIDDLE YEARS: AGES 9-11

The ages six to twelve are commonly known as the middle years of childhood. This is the time when children are in full bloom; they are no longer babies but the demands of adult life are still far away. All through this period children continue to develop their special personalities. They are getting to know more about themselves and the world in which they live and their slow steady growth can be observed. They grow in independence and become more able to take care of themselves. They also are eager adventurers who learn from their explorations but who often find, to their dismay and to the dismay of the adults around them, that they still have a lot to learn.

Each child is different and there are no set rules for rearing or teaching children. How children grow depends on the characteristics they inherit from their parents and, to a good extent, it depends on the guidance provided by parents and other adults. It also depends on the experiences youngsters have inside and outside of their homes.

Although each child's temperament makes her special, certain guidelines of child growth apply to most youngsters, and parents and other caregivers may find these guidelines helpful when working with the middle-years child.

- **In physical development,** height and weight increase slowly and evenly. Children gain about two or three inches in height each year. Body proportions also change. In contrast to the chunky body of the preschooler, during the middle years the trunk becomes slimmer, the chest becomes broader, and the arms and legs thin out.
- **In psychological development,** middle-years children can find themselves in conflict between the need to grow up and the

desire to remain a child forever. They want to grow up so that they can enjoy the prerogatives of adult life, but they also want to hold on to all the privileges of childhood.

During the middle years, boys and girls gradually become aware of sexual differences. Fortunately, children now are encouraged to try activities traditionally reserved for the opposite sex-a trend that is helping to break down sex-role stereotypes.

• **In social development,** the middle-years child may appear to be a staid traditionalist who accepts the authority of the family. The family is the main base of security and identity, although around the age of eleven the child begins to place more and more value on the peer group.

Ages and Stages

The information presented here about the ages and stages of children is only a *guide*. Physically, emotionally, and intellectually, each child grows and develops at his own rate. Some youngsters may be early bloomers. That is, they may have reached a stage of emotional or physical development beyond their chronological years. Understanding the characteristics of an age can be helpful to adults who work with or care for children. But, if adults are to foster optimal growth and development in children, they also must remain sensitive and responsive to children as individuals.

Nine-Year-Olds
General
Nine is a developmental middle zone.

• The nine-year-old shows a new maturity, self-confidence, and independence from adults.

• There is an increase in maturity and refinement of behavior. Judgmental tendencies are more discerning and objective. Nine-year-olds can evaluate themselves, find that they are lacking, but not feel guilty about it.

Self-Concept and Independence
• Nine-year-olds tend to be inner-directed and self-motivated.

• They have occasions of intense emotion and impatience, but their outbursts are less frequent and they show greater self-control. The inner-directed quality of their behavior allows nine-year-olds to become intently involved in activities.

• If forced to interrupt an activity, nine-year-olds will usually come back to it on their own.

• They can think and reason for themselves.

• They can be trusted.

• They may withdraw from surroundings to get a sense of self. They do not, however, retreat as much as they did when they were seven.

• Nine-year-olds do not feel impelled to boast and attack to protect themselves.

Relating to Other Children and Adults
• In their relationships with both adults and peers, they show consideration and fairness beyond that shown at a younger age.

• They can accept their own failures and mistakes, and they are willing to take responsibility for their own actions.

• Nine-year-olds have an increased awareness of sex and sex-differentiated behaviors.

• Girls can become concerned about their clothing and appearance. They take more interest in the "right" fashion.

• Friendships tend to be more solid, but occasionally nine-year-olds can have an intense dislike of the opposite sex, preferring to be with children of their own age and sex. Boys and girls both may begin to form clubs around various activities.

• Although their independence can be trying at times, they are often easier to work with than younger children who make great demands on adults.

• They are anxious to please and love to be chosen.

- Most of the mother-child conflict of the eight-year-old has disappeared, and the nine-year-old makes fewer demands on parents.
- Nine-year-olds usually have no problems with young children or older brothers and sisters. In fact, they can be very loyal to siblings.

Games and Activities
- Nine-year-olds spend much time in solitary activities of their own choosing.
- Bicycling, roller and ice skating, and swimming are physical activities they enjoy.
- They continue to enjoy the advanced table games they learned at eight.
- Materials and information attract the nine-year-old. Organized games or activities such as baseball, football, and basketball are popular. Many children at this age also have mastered basic reading and arithmetic and can use these skills to gain information, to solve problems, and to participate in games and recreation.

Ten-Year-Olds

General
Ten is the high point of childhood. Ten-year-olds have worked through the difficulties of home, school, and community. They now can take pride in their ability to fit in at home, at school, and at play with their peers. On occasion, there can be outbursts of anger, depression, or sadness, but these moods are short-lived and soon forgotten.
- Girls are slightly more advanced sexually than boys and already there is some evidence of the rapid sprint to maturity that will make them taller and heavier than boys their own age in a couple of years. Their bodies are rounding out and the softening of contours may begin. Some girls may even experience the first stages of breast development. Girls become concerned about their bodies and menstruation and about sexual activity in general.
- For boys physical changes are less marked, thus concern for the body and physical maturity is much less noticeable.

Self-Concept and Independence
- Ten-year-olds accept themselves as they are without worrying too much about their strengths and weaknesses. They are much less interested in evaluating themselves. They like their bodies and like what they can do both athletically and academically. Their self-acceptance is heightened by the acceptance accorded them by peers, families, and school.

Relating to Other Children and Adults
- Ten-year-olds like and enjoy their friends. Boys may move into loosely organized groups. Within these groups, boys may have particular friends, but there is a lot of switching around. Girls usually move in smaller groups and are likely to form more intense friendships and have more serious "falling outs" with their friends being "mad" and "not playing" or "not speaking" to one another as a result. There are times when ten-year-olds may seem to value their peer group more than their families.
- Teachers and other adults who interact with this age group are popular if they are fair and not partial to particular children in the group. Adults working with ten-year-olds need to be firm but not strict. At this age children like adult leaders to schedule activities and like to keep to the schedule.

Games and Activities
- They like outings and trips.
- They like organized games and belonging to clubs and groups.
- When working on a project they may need to get up and move about.

Eleven-Year-Olds

General

At this age, there is an accelerated growth pace.

• The eleven-year-old's activity level increases; energy and appetite also increase.

• There is a tendency at this age to forget manners, to be loud, rude, and boorish, and to take unnecessary chances as a means of defying adult authority. Riding bicycles in heavy traffic is an example of this kind of behavior.

• Eleven-year-olds quarrel a good deal with adults and lack emotional control although they can be cooperative and friendly with strangers. They need firmness and understanding from adults.

Self-Concept and Independence

• They can be belligerent because of their high energy level, which pushes them toward activities, but which sometimes leads to carelessness.

• The eleven-year-old is looking for new self-definition.

• They will often confront others with criticism in an effort to get attention. They can, however, admit faults.

• They will sometimes differ with parents on careers and have dreams of being famous while their parents try to temper such fantasies.

• An eleven-year-old, on occasion, will challenge parents and other adults on child-rearing practices.

Relating to Other Children and Adults

• Boys and girls have best friends and a group of other friends who are selected because of common interests and temperaments.

• Both boys and girls admit to being interested in the opposite sex and show their interest by teasing, joking, and showing off.

• Eleven-year-olds like to quarrel with others, but don't like others to argue with them.

• They can be cooperative, friendly, and pleasant with adults, but they need to be treated with understanding and firmness.

• Eleven-year-olds can feel left out from their peer group.

Games and Activities

• They don't like to work with materials that are complex, but they do like things that show off their rote skills.

• Eleven-year-olds have trouble understanding relationships and the complex combinations of events.

In Summary

Children are individuals with their own special temperaments and idiosyncracies. The ages and stages children go through can vary tremendously from one child to the next and, by respecting the variousness of children, parents and other caregivers can help them develop strong and healthy self-concepts.

III - ADOLESCENTS

> *The young are prone to desire and in regard to sexual desire they exercise no self-restraint. They are changeful, too, and fickle in their desires. They are passionate, irascible, and apt to be carried away by their impulses. They are slaves, too, of their passion.*

A distinguished scientist and philosopher made this observation over 2000 years ago. To some, Aristotle's lament might suggest that adolescents haven't changed much since the days of ancient Athens, but recent research indicates that what hasn't changed is adults' *perceptions* of adolescents. Surveys of adolescents and their parents show that their values and attitudes are generally quite compatible. The famous "generation gap" appears to be an invention of the news media in response to a small but highly visible group of adolescents whose challenge to the older generation in the 1960s was mistakenly interpreted as representative.

What is it about the stage of life between childhood and adulthood that makes it so difficult for adults to understand? Although adolescence is not equally troublesome in all societies and for all families, adults' reports of its stressful nature are sufficiently widespread to warrant attention.

Change-physical, mental, and social change-is the most notable quality of adolescence and accounts for a good deal of the difficulty.

Physical Changes

The most obvious physical change during adolescence is rapid acceleration of growth. Within two years before or after age 12 for girls and age 14 for boys, a growth spurt occurs. The rate of gain in height and weight typically doubles for a year or more. Physical growth takes place in a fairly consistent sequence, beginning at the extremities and moving inward. Head, hands, and feet enlarge first, followed by arms and legs, then trunk. The broadening of male shoulders and female hips that characterizes adult body form occurs last. Overall growth is accompanied, though not always in the same order or at the same rate, by maturation of the reproductive organs and glands and by the appearance of pubic and underarm hair, and facial hair in males.

Together, these physical changes accomplish the biological aspect of adolescence, which is known as pubescence: they transform a child into an adult, one who is able to have children.

But this physical transformation is not as simple for the person going through it as it sounds when described in the abstract. For one thing, the ages at which pubescence begins and is completed vary as much as four years among different young people. Furthermore, the period from beginning to completion may be as little as 18 months for some and as much as six years for others. As a result of this variation, any group of early adolescents is likely to include young people who are at very different points in pubescence. Because girls enter pubescence, on the average, two years earlier than boys, the greatest variation among girls' physical maturation occurs during ages 11-13, while in boys it is during ages 13-15.

Rapid change combined with wide variation among individuals tend to make adolescents extremely sensitive to their appearance. At no other time in life are feelings about the self (self-esteem) so closely tied to feelings about the body (body image). Physical appearance also affects the ways in which other people treat an adolescent. Adults tend to expect adult behavior from a 15-year-old boy who is six feet tall and shaves regularly, but they will readily excuse childish behavior on the part of his classmate who, though the same age, has not yet begun his growth spurt. Perhaps even more importantly, peers judge one another on the basis of physical size and appearance. Early maturation can be an advantage for boys but often is not for girls because it puts them out-of-step with their peers.

The physical changes of pubescence, therefore, have direct effects on adolescents' social relations. They also affect emotions. The maturation of the gonads reproductive glandschanges the balance of hormones in the body, which can result in new sensitivities to the environment. For example, an adolescent may have a heightened sensitivity to loss of sleep, which results in moodiness or outbursts of temper. Cyclical changes in hormonal balance, especially among girls but also to some extent among boys, are associated with changes in emotions, behavior, and thinking. Since these cycles are new to adolescents, they may not be handled well.

Mental Changes

The most important mental change during adolescence is the growth in capacity for abstract thinking. Before age 11 or 12, children think in terms of concrete objects and groups of objects. Their reasoning is simple and direct. It does not allow for much complexity or subtlety. Given a problem to solve, the child tends to plunge into it with first one possible solution and then another until she either finds the correct solution or gives up. Confronted with a moral dilemma, she responds on the basis of a rule, which may or may not be appropriately applied.

By age 16, most adolescents have transcended this simple way of thinking, though not all of them adopt the most complex forms of reasoning. Nor do all use the same types of reasoning about all issues, any more than adults do. Adolescents begin to achieve the capacity to approach a problem systematically. Instead of moving immediately into the trying out of an assortment of solutions, they can analyze the problem and arrive at some tentative conclusions about what sorts of solutions probably will and will not work. Then they can proceed in a logical fashion to test and evaluate solutions, gaining a greater understanding of the problem along the way.

Moral issues become much more complex than they are for young children because adolescents are able to understand that two sound rules or principles might conflict in some cases. For example, they will understand that in certain situations, the values of friendship and honesty conflict, and they will struggle with a question about whether someone should report a friend for breaking a rule. Younger children are more likely to choose either one principle or the other without recognizing the dilemma. Furthermore, adolescents outgrow the childish belief that only evil people do bad things. They understand accident and circumstances involve even the best-intentioned people in undesirable actions. They are, therefore, likely to be more understanding and forgiving of human frailty than young children, though their interest in principles can also make adolescents morally rigid at times.

Along with the capacity to think abstractly comes the realization that what exists is only one of many possibilities. Thinking about those possibilities becomes a fascinating activity. The real is frequently compared to the ideal and found wanting. Because they can conceive of a more ideal worJd without having to bother themselves with all the details of how it might be achieved and what drawbacks it might have, adolescents are often impatient with the real world and with the failure of adults to have made it better already.

This capacity to think about many possible realities is important, given the momentous choices adolescents will make as they move into adulthood and choose career directions, educational paths, and mates. Without it they are likely to drift into the first opportunities that arise without considering what the other possibilities might be, which are most desirable, and which are feasible.

Similarly, the ability to reason about moral issues is necessary if a person is to establish a personal moral code. Rules and principles simply accepted from parents and other authorities are essential to children, but adolescents need to think through rules and principles and consider the alternatives in order to adopt or adapt them for themselves. An adolescent who does not go through the process of questioning principles and values may be without guidance when confronted with a new and complex moral dilemma or when one or another of his/her basic principles is seriously challenged.

Social Changes

Because of their physical and mental growth, adolescents are no longer treated like children. The expectations adults and peers have of them change and their behavior changes. Thus the social world in which they live changes in important ways.

One of the most obvious social changes is the initiation of serious interest in and interactions with young people of the opposite sex. The physical and emotional changes of pubescence described above lead to strong new feelings between girls and boys. Even before they begin to act upon these feelings by dating and engaging in other heterosexual activities, many adolescents begin to have "crushes" on opposite-sex peers, and sometimes on same-sex peers and on adults. These one-way emotional attachments simply indicate the presence of new emotional capacities, but they can be difficult for the adolescent to understand and deal with. Learning to handle the emotions and behavior that go along with attracting and forming emotional attachments to members of the opposite sex can be stressful, in addition to being terribly exciting.

The social world of the adolescent changes in other ways as well. A sixteen-year-old may notice that adults are treating her more like one of them, engaging in real conversation, for example, instead of saying "My, how you've grown," and asking about school. She may also notice that she enjoys this adult conversation when just a year or two before she would have preferred to go out and play.

By the age of sixteen, adolescents are being given many privileges formerly reserved for adults. In most places they can drive a car, quit school, and hold a job. Although it is usually against the law, they can fairly easily smoke and drink alcoholic beverages.

Relations with parents change too. As they grow more mature, adolescents are less dependent on their parents than they were earlier. They might be able to live on their own. They have ideas of their own and are reconsidering some of the beliefs and values their parents have taught them. They receive emotional support from peers. Sometimes their peers' values are inconsistent with their parents'. For all these reasons, they become less deferent to their parents' wishes and opinions, adopting a more independent and often a more aggressive stance.

Modern industrial societies demand highly educated workers and do not need the labor of children. Therefore, most young people experience a long gap between the attainment of physical adulthood and adult status. Marriage, parenthood, and full-time paid employment are the principal indicators of adult status in our society. At least two ambiguities arise from this social definition of adulthood. One is that young people are expected to postpone marriage and to remain economically dependent on their parents for several years after they are physically capable of reproduction and full-time employment. A second is that while many young people "prolong their adolescence" by enrolling in college and then in graduate or professional school, many of their peers are entering full-time employment, getting married, and starting families. Although adolescence can be an enjoyable stage of life because of the freedom from adult obligations, it can also be a frustrating time because adult privileges are withheld.

Difficulties for Parents

Adolescents are no longer children; they and their parents have to work out new ways of dealing with each other that recognize their growing but not yet complete maturity. Parents must realize that they can no longer control their offspring in many important areas. Adolescents simply have too many opportunities to do as they please. Young people, who are often adamant in demanding relief from parental control, need to understand that freedom demands responsibility. They cannot expect their parents to give them adult privileges regarding their social activities and then excuse them from household obligations because they are only children.

One of the reasons adolescents often seem to be a burden to their parents is that parents have to change the way they treat their adolescents. Parental behavior that has developed over several years and has been rather effective becomes obsolete. New behavior, a new parental style, is called for.

Being required to deal with new challenges and to behave in different ways is always difficult, but it can be especially difficult for parents of adolescents who are simultaneously experiencing stress in other parts of their lives. The term "midlife crisis" has become popular in recent years in recognition that many people go through a period of self-examination and often of serious readjustment in middle age as they realize they have relatively few years left to accomplish what they aspire to. Two life cycle changes in the family are associated with this midlife crisis: one is the death of one's own parents and the other is the maturation of one's children. People at this point frequently have to accept the fact that they will not achieve the prominence in their careers that they might have wanted. Common responses to this "crisis" include career and marital changes.

Parents who are experiencing crises of this magnitude are likely to feel overwhelmed by the challenges of dealing with their rapidly changing adolescents. But even parents who feel satisfied and secure in most aspects of their lives may have difficulty coping with their adolescent children.

What Adults Can Do for Adolescents

There are times when the adolescent says, "Why don't you just leave me alone!" and the adult wants to say, "Alright, I will." That is not a solution, however, because adolescents need adults to help them achieve adulthood themselves. The following suggestions may prove helpful to adults who work with adolescents, but they cannot be treated as a cookbook. Just as adolescents refuse to follow many adult "recipes" for proper behavior because they need to work out their own behavioral code, adults must be flexible and resourceful in responding to adolescents. There is no single way to do it.

1. Be honest. With their newly developed capacity for abstract thinking, adolescents become fascinated with principles and with consistency. They are severe critics of adults they think are hypocritical or two-faced. Most adolescents are sophisticated enough to see through dishonesty or pretention in adults who are close to them. They tend to be skeptical at what adults tell them and to welcome any confirmation of that skepticism.

2. Be open. Adolescents want and need to talk about things with their parents and other adults close to them. But they also need to maintain their privacy and their independence. Therefore, adult-adolescent conversations cannot be one-sided, with the adolescent baring his soul and the adult listening and offering advice. Adolescents need to know that some of the same concerns they struggle with are concerns of adults too.

Sexuality is one of the most insistent concerns of adolescents because it is a new one, brought out by their sexual maturation. Adults cannot be very helpful to adolescents about sexual issues unless they, as adults, are comfortable with their own sexuality. They must be willing to acknowledge the complexity of the issues and the strength of the social and emotional pressures. In our society the "official" morality is that sexual relations are limited to marriage, yet television, movies, magazines, songs on the radio, and even billboards bombard us constantly with the message that sexual attractiveness is the most important personal quality and that unrestrained sexual behavior is good. Like adolescents, adults can find this contradiction confusing, and they should be willing to discuss it.

3. Set clear and consistent limits. Most children will abide by rules their parents or other adults set down just because they are rules, at least as long as the adult is looking. Adolescents are much more likely to want to know why a particular rule or expectation has been stated. Adults should respect this need for explanation and should allow for some negotiation regarding rules for behavior. But, consistent with the recommendation to be honest, adults should not hesitate to say what they believe is absolutely essential and is not open to negotiation.

There may be some rules or limits set by parents that adolescents continue to violate because they are independent enough to do so. Parents may have to acknowledge that they cannot control what the adolescent does away from home but make clear that they will not allow it in the home and then follow through with that prohibition.

4. Remember that growing up means becoming independent. Effective parents, and other adults who succeed in helping adolescents become adults, are able to accept young people making choices that they would not have made and behaving in ways they do not approve of. That is what independence means. Young adults who still do as they are told all the time are immature and unprepared to face a world in which they are constantly required to decide for themselves. Most adolescents become adults who are a source of pride and happiness for their parents and for the other adults who worked with them. But for this to happen, they must first establish some independence, and that can require a painful break.

Adolescents undergo dramatic physical and mental changes in a short period of time, and they are given a confusing in-between place in our society. The period can be painful for the adolescents and for the adults who are close to them. But it is a necessary process both for the adolescents to come of age and for our society to renew itself through the questions, the new perspective, and the new talents that each group of young people brings into adulthood.

www.ingramcontent.com/pod-product-compliance
Lightning Source LLC
Chambersburg PA
CBHW082046300426
44117CB00015B/2624